100 Ideas for Teaching Problem Solving,
Reasoning and Numeracy

Continuum One Hundreds Series

100 Ideas for Teaching Communication, Language and Literacy – Susan Elkin

100 Ideas for Teaching Knowledge and Understanding of the World – Alan Thwaites

100 Ideas for Teaching Creative Development – Wendy Bowkett and Stephen Bowkett

100 Ideas for Developing Good Practice in the Early Years – Wendy Bowkett and Stephen Bowkett

100 + Ideas for Managing Behaviour – Johnnie Young

100 + Ideas for Teaching Creativity – Stephen Bowkett

100 + Ideas for Teaching Mathematics – Mike Ollerton

100 + Ideas for Teaching Thinking Skills – Stephen Bowkett

100 + Ideas for Teaching English – Angella Cooze

100 + Ideas for Teaching History – Julia Murphy

100 Ideas for Surviving Your First Year in Teaching – Laura-Jane Fisher

100 Ideas for Trainee Teachers – Angella Cooze

100 Ideas for Teaching Citizenship – Ian Davies

100 Ideas for Supply Teachers – Julia Murphy

100 Ideas for Teaching Science – Sharon Archer

100 Ideas for Teaching Geography – Andy Leeder

100 Ideas for Primary Supply Teachers – Michael Parry

100 Ideas for Essential Teaching Skills – Neal Watkin and Johannes Ahrenfelt

100 Ideas for Primary Assemblies – Fred Sedgwick

100 Ideas for Teaching Writing – Anthony Haynes

100 Ideas for Lesson Planning – Anthony Haynes

100 Ideas for Secondary School Assemblies – Susan Elkin

100 Ideas for Teaching Drama – Johnnie Young

100 Ideas for Developing Thinking in the Primary School – Fred Sedgwick

100 Ideas for Teaching

Problem Solving, Reasoning and Numeracy

Alan Thwaites

continuum

Continuum International Publishing Group

The Tower Building
11 York Road
London
SE1 7NX

80 Maiden Lane
Suite 704
New York
NY 10038

www.continuumbooks.com

British Library Cataloguing-in-Publication Data
A catalogue record for this book is available from the British Library.

ISBN: 9-780-8264-9905-9 (paperback)

Designed and typeset by Kenneth Burnley, Wirral, Cheshire
Printed and bound in Great Britain by Cromwell Press Ltd., Trowbridge, Wiltshire

Contents

Section 3: 16–26 months

Section 4: 22–36 months

Section 5: 30–50 months

Section 6: 40–60+ months

Health and Safety Note

We advise that all of the ideas in this book be carried out under adult supervision, with the art activities especially being closely supervised. As a pre-school practitioner you know your children and should judge which ones are capable of doing which activities for themselves, or where and how much adult help with equipment is needed. Wear protective clothing such as apron and gloves when handling dyes, etc. Do not allow children to use irons. If using sprays ensure windows are open. Be aware of children with allergies and asthma when using paints, fibres, chalk and sand, etc.

Acknowledgements

Many thanks to Judith Thwaites for her invaluable ideas, encouragement and proofreading.

Also, many thanks to Penny Tassoni, without whom this would not have been possible.

Thank you Maplehurst Nursery, Hastings.

References

The Statutory Framework for the Early Years Foundation Stage (EYFS) is obtainable as a download from: www.standards.dfes.gov.uk and www.publications.teachernet.gov.uk.

The DfES *'Birth to Three Matters'* is obtainable from: www.surestart.gov.uk

Introduction

Children acquire many sophisticated skills and abilities before commencing full-time education, making their pre-school experiences vital for their future education. The ground rules for life are laid in the first years. Provision for the care of those aged 0–5 years can vary upon parental circumstances and wishes and there are similar variations in the type of care available outside the home. A child beginning primary education who has received good quality care and learning experiences, whether that be entirely at home or with a combination of various early years providers, will be confident and eager to learn.

Using numbers; shapes, space and measures; sorting and matching are all enjoyable activities for young children. We have all enjoyed the rhythm and here-it-comes effect of counting rhymes and songs. Young children love the sense of achievement in completing match-the-shape puzzles and sorting games, and that pleasure does not diminish in old age. The fun of playing with numbers and shapes builds a body of knowledge and skills. It enables problem solving and the desire to ask new questions. It connects to other areas of learning and development. This book offers numeracy activities for pre-school care providers wishing to capitalize on the enthusiasm of the children and their desire to learn.

Using this book

If you enjoy using this book then so will the children in your care. The ideas have been chosen for their enjoyment and play value. The need for elaborate or expensive resources has been kept to a minimum. Ideas for extension or innovation are included where appropriate. Childcare providers are obviously very aware of health and safety issues but it is hoped none will be offended if a health and safety note may be included with many of the ideas. The intention has been, first of all, to provide a user-friendly set of activities with a real value to the children.

There is no recommended or even suggested duration for any of the ideas. Clearly, this will depend upon the age, stage of development and, above all, the interest of the children. Some ideas stand alone but many are designed to be worked in with the regular sessions and routines of the day. It is assumed also that any activity, once started, would be modified or changed altogether should the enjoyment level be lost. It is very likely that any given idea will work one day but not another or will work for one child but not another. It is expected that practitioners will enjoy adapting and innovating and will place their own personal stamp upon the interaction with the children in their care.

It is not the purpose of this book to go into great detail about the Early Years Foundation Stage (EYFS) Framework, briefly described below. It is assumed all early years care providers will have had access to it and familiarized themselves with the requirements. However, the ideas suggested in these pages are designed to assist with meeting the requirements of the EYFS and can be directly linked to the aspects and age groups set out in it.

The sections are arranged in the broad age groups of the EYFS. These age groups overlap somewhat, allowing for obvious variations in development. It is expected that the groupings will be used merely as a rough guide.

Most of the ideas included for younger children can be used throughout all the age-ranges, either as they stand or with minor modification. Thus, it will be possible to use almost all of the ideas with children who are aged 4–5 years. Young children love to play favourite games and sing favourite songs over and over again. It builds confidence as well as knowledge and skills.

With each of the 100 ideas there is a reference to the relevant EYFS Problem Solving, Reasoning and Numeracy aspect or, in many cases, more than one aspect.

Statutory Framework for the Early Years Foundation Stage (EYFS)

Provision for pre-school children in its widest sense has, for the first time, been brought together by the DfES within its *Statutory Framework for the Early Years Foundation Stage* (EYFS) 2007. The expectation is that the body of skills, abilities and knowledge outlined in the Framework will be developed through essentially enjoyable play activities and experiences within daily routines. Very young children, especially, need to learn and discover through enjoyment and play at their own pace.

The Problem Solving, Reasoning and Numeracy Programme (EYFS)

Learning and Development, according to the Framework, covers six areas or programmes: i) Personal, Social and Emotional Development; ii) Communication, Language and Literacy; iii) Problem Solving, Reasoning and Numeracy; iv) Knowledge and Understanding of the World; v) Physical Development; and vi) Creative Development. Each of these areas is further divided into aspects of learning, the number of these varying between programmes. This book is concerned with the Problem Solving, Reasoning and Numeracy programme but there will inevitably be overlaps with other programmes.

Aspect of Learning	. . . is about
Numbers as Labels and for Counting	Recognizing the shapes of different numbers and how to say them
	Learning to count
	Naming things around you
	Making sense of signs
Calculating	Logical thinking
	Recognizing equal amounts, more and less
Shape, Space and Measures	Recognizing basic shapes and naming them
	Forming ideas of place, size, distance, weight, volume and capacity

Section 1:
Birth–11 months

Children of this age soak up all the messages and signals that all their senses
experience. Full understanding of what they hear, see, touch, smell and taste
will come through the security of constant contact, repetition and enjoyment.
Most of these first ideas should be developed into the older age groups as
independence grows.

Having a Ball

EYFS Aspect	Resources	Group Size
Numbers as Labels and for Counting Shape, Space and Measures	Collection of soft and hard balls of different colours, easily gripped by child	1 or 2 children

- Play a game of rolling a favourite ball to and fro. This can be played at the start to stimulate interest, during to maintain interest, and to round off.

- Give the child the balls to hold, feel, smell and so on, describing them all the time.

- Use the vocabulary: round – smooth – fluffy – squashy – hard.

- Divide the balls into groups by colour, explaining what you are doing all the time.

- Count each colour slowly, involving the child, e.g. holding their hand to divide the balls.

- Divide the balls into groups by texture or size and count again – also very slowly, involving the child all the time.

Taking this further

Any collection of shapes can be used but the variations in size, shape and texture should not be too wide. The younger members of this age group will have less developed manipulative skills, but a 10–11 month old may well be able to respond to questions like, 'Where is the red ball?' by indicating or grabbing. Ensure that the surface of each ball is safe and cannot be chewed or licked off.

Safety Note

No ball should be small enough to be swallowed.

IDEA 2

Have a Nappy Time

EYFS Aspect	*Resources*	*Group Size*
Numbers as Labels and for Counting	Baby changing paraphernalia	Individual

● This can make a routine event more fun. The little one may not be very responsive in a soiled or wet nappy but once all the cleaning up is done it is the ideal time for a little sensory game with numbers thrown in.

● As you do up the buttons or poppers, count them in a little chant, 'One little button, two little buttons', and so on.

● Do the same with washed fingers or toes (just one hand or foot), tweaking them as you count and finish with 'Two ears and a nose'.

● Repeat with your own fingers, ears and nose for the child to watch and wait expectantly for their turn to come again.

Taking this further

Nappy change, like any other quality one-to-one time is a good opportunity for any sensory games like 'Round and round the garden like a teddy bear'. The number of steps can be increased with age.

Now You See It, Now You Don't

EYFS Aspect	Resources	Group Size
Shape, Space and Measures	Two cushions – one round and one square A favourite toy	1 or 2 children

This is based upon peek-a-boo games.

- Play along with the child and a favourite toy – we'll call it 'teddy' – to arouse interest.

- Holding one of the cushions, say the round one, move the teddy behind it, making sure the child sees where it goes.

- Say 'Where's teddy?' – pause for effect – then, making teddy peep out, 'Behind the . . . ROUND cushion!'

- Repeat two or three times and then repeat with the square cushion.

- Use both cushions and alternate disappearance and reappearance so baby experiences the surprise factor when teddy goes behind round and comes out from the square and vice versa. It is essential that the toy is played with between disappearances in order to maintain interest.

 Taking this further

As the manipulative skills of the child develop he/she may be able to do his/her own hiding for the adult.

Make-a-Pair

EYFS Aspect	Resources	Group Size
Calculating	None	Individual

This is another one of those sensory games for a cosy one-to-one time, played with the child on the lap or in a bouncy chair.

- Play with the feet and say, '[child's name]'s got a pair of feet . . . and they're for . . . walking' [make walking movements with child's feet].

- Play with the knees and say, '[child's name]'s got a pair of knees . . . and they're for . . . knocking' [gently knock the knees together].

- Do the same with: hands (clapping); arms (waving); ears (wiggling); eyes (blinking); shoes (stamping); gloves (warming).

- At some point – not necessarily after going right through the child's pairs – the adult does their own pairs. '[Adult's name]'s got a pair of feet' and so on.

Taking this further
The favourite soft toy can be involved as well.

IDEA 5

Story Time

EYFS Aspect	Resources	Group Size
Numbers as Labels and for Counting	Any good first numbers picture book	1 or 2 children

This is one where the resource, i.e. the book you choose, decides the enjoyment value of the experience.

For very young children the greatest impact will be with cloth books or those which include feely pages. Certainly, bright colourful pictures of familiar animals and objects are a must.

The adult engages the child by talking through the pictures – adding sound effects and actions where possible – essentially emphasizing the number elements.

IDEA 6

Sing-a-Song 1: London Bridge

EYFS Aspect	Resources	Group Size
Numbers for Labels and for Counting	None	1 or 2 children

- Sing this song to the tune of *London Bridge is Falling Down*:

  [Child's name] has got one nose, got one nose, got one nose [touch child's nose],
  [Child's name] has got one nose,
  That's for smelling.
  Scrunch it up and make it sniff, make it sniff, make it sniff [wrinkle nose and sniff],
  Scrunch it up and make it sniff,
  Uuhhmmm, what's for dinner?

  [Child's name] has got two ears, got two ears, got two ears [tweak the ears],
  [Child's name] has got two ears,
  They're for hearing.
  Listen to me whispering, whispering, whispering [move closer and closer to child's ear, singing],
  Listen to me whispering, (quieter and quieter as you go),
  What's for dinner?

- Make up your own for:

  Two hands/They're for clapping/Come along and clap with me/Clap, clap, cla..ap;
  Two legs/They're for walking/Come along and walk with me/Stomp, stomp, sto..omp;
  Five toes/They're for tickling/I am going to tickle your toes/Tickle, tickle, tickle.

- On the same lines, here is a rhyme you might like to add (it can be sung, but not to the same tune):

  Two little eyes to look around,
  Two little ears to hear each sound,
  One little nose to smell what's sweet,
  One little mouth that likes to eat.

IDEA

7

Build It Up

EYFS Aspect	Resources	Group Size
All	Building bricks	1 or 2 children (who can sit up confidently)

This can be done as part of a general 'playing with bricks' session.

- Sit with the children and play along with the building.

- Count the bricks as they go up, using the vocabulary:

  One, Two, Three, and so on;

  Bigger; taller; higher; how many bricks are there?

- To make the game more exciting and therefore more memorable, express excitement as it grows and mild shock when it falls.

- Make a game out of knocking it down.

Safety Note

Take care when knocking down the bricks and discourage throwing.

IDEA 8

Sing-a-Song 2: If You're Happy

EYFS Aspect	Resources	Group Size
Numbers for Labels and for Counting Shape, Space and Measures	Set of similar objects/toys (optional)	1–3 children

To the tune of *If You're Happy and You Know It, Clap Your Hands*.

The child(ren) needs to be facing the adult, either sitting confidently or in a bouncer.

Make the actions very clear as you sing the words:

Verse 1

If you're happy and you know it, clap your hands [clap twice].
(Repeat)
If you're happy and you know it, then you really ought to show it.
If you're happy and you know it, clap your hands [clap twice].

Verse 2

If you're happy and you know it, count to two [clap twice, saying 1, 2 as you go].
(Repeat)
If you're happy and you know it, then you really ought to show it.
If you're happy and you know it, count to two [clap twice, saying 1,2 as you go].

Verse 3

If you're happy . . . make a circle ['draw' a large circle in the air with hands].

Verse 4

If you're happy . . . make a square ['draw' a large square in the air with hands].

> ## Taking this further
>
> **Any actions can be used, e.g. nod your head, touch your nose, stamp your feet (for those able to stand), touch the sky. For consistency, it is good to try to keep any repetitions of actions to two.**
>
> **NB: Older children can add in each action, counting longer in groups of two.**

Section 2:
8–20 months

Any of the ideas in the previous section could be used for this age group. It is around this age that children begin to really appreciate nursery rhymes. They are invaluable for presenting a whole range of early concepts, including those associated with number. Their importance can easily be overlooked and early years teachers in primary schools regularly bemoan the fact that children arrive with very little knowledge of them. A number are included here.

Bowling Alley

YFS Aspect	Resources	Group Size
Numbers as Labels and for Counting Shape, Space and Measures	Lightweight ball and several skittles or light objects for knocking over	1 or 2 children (who can sit up confidently)

For these very young children they may seem to be incidental in the game and will need a lot of help but it is great fun. It is not too soon to begin to develop the concepts of distance and force as well as number.

● Set up a bowling alley with five or six skittles or similar targets.

● Find a suitable distance to bowl from.

● Knock down the skittles either with a roll or a throw.

Vary the game with distance and spread of the skittles depending on age and ability.

If there are two children then this is an ideal opportunity for introducing the notion of taking turns.

Taking this further

For older children, give a challenge to aim for the 'red one' or the 'one at the end' or 'in between' and include the counting of knocked or missed skittles.

Safety Note

Targets should not be breakable and the ball must be soft and light.

Two's Company

EYFS Aspect	Resources	Group Size
All	A range of pairs, e.g. shoes, gloves, socks	1–3 children

- Show the selection of pairs and talk about them, emphasizing the relationship between 'pair' and 'two'.

- Remove one of each of the pairs and spread them out within easy reach.

- Ask one child at a time to match the pairs together again. They could do the whole set or take it in turns to match a single pair.

Taking this further

- Try including an odd item with a pair, e.g. three identical socks to introduce the concept of 'odd'.

- Spread out many socks or other paired items and challenge the children to match them up.

How Many Hiding?

This activity will be better managed by the older children in this age group.

EYFS Aspect	Resources	Group Size
Numbers as Labels and for Counting	Up to five toys or familiar objects Three cloths each painted with large, clear, colourful spots – one with a single spot, one with two spots and one with three	1–3 children

- Begin by playing with a few toys.

- At a convenient point, select a toy, say a car, and cover it with the single-spot cloth.

- Ask, 'What's under there?' 'Is it the [another toy]?' 'No' and so on.

- Point out the single spot before revealing or the child reveals.

- Play with the car and any other toy to maintain interest.

- Move on to hide two toys, covered with the two-spot cloth.

- Use the same suspense-building before the reveal.

- Point out the two spots and relate it to the two toys.

- Have another short play and then repeat with three toys and the three-spot cloth.

Taking this further

Encourage the child to hide the toys for you to guess what is underneath.

This Little Pig

EYFS Aspect	Resources	Group Size
Numbers as Labels and for Counting Calculating	None	1–3 children . . . traditionally 1-to-1 while drying the feet

Say the nursery rhyme, *This Little Pig* with actions:

> This little pig went to market [tweak thumb or big toe],
> This little pig stayed at home [tweak first finger or toe],
> This little pig had roast beef [tweak middle finger or toe],
> This little pig had none [tweak third finger or toe],
> And this little pig cried, Squeak! Squeak! Squeak! All the way home.

[Tweak the little finger or toe and tickle up the tummy to chin.]

This will stand on its own with the younger children in the age range. The child will want it repeated over and over again on both hands and both feet. For those at the end of the age range it is worth pointing out that they are actually counting on their fingers by asking 'How many pigs is that?' before counting each finger, 1–5. Also, asking the question, 'How many are left?' will introduce an early stage of understanding number bonds.

Taking this further

Incorporate it into a game with farm – or any other – animals. They do not have to be all the same.

IDEA 13

Hickory Dickory Dock

EYFS Aspect	Resources	Group Size
Numbers as Labels and for Counting Shape, Space and Measures	Teaching clock and a toy mouse – perhaps a finger puppet mouse (optional)	1–3 children

This works well either with the child on the lap, using the fingers as the mouse to perform the actions, or with a toy mouse and a toy clock.

Either way, tell the rhyme:

> Hickory dickory dock,
> The mouse ran up the clock [walk fingers up tummy or mouse up clock],
> The clock struck one [DING],
> The mouse ran down [run fingers down tummy or mouse down clock],
> Hickory dickory dock.

Verse 2

> Hickory dickory dock,
> The mouse ran up the clock [actions as before],
> The clock struck two [DING – DING],
> The mouse then flew [fingers or mouse 'fly' away],
> Hickory dickory dock.

Verse 3

> Hickory dickory dock,
> The mouse ran up the clock [actions as before],
> The clock struck three [DING – DING – DING],
> The mouse laughed, hee, hee [tickle the tummy/wobble mouse with a chuckle],
> Hickory dickory dock.

Verse 4

Hickory dickory dock,
The mouse ran up the clock [actions as before],
The clock struck four [DING – DING – DING – DING],
The mouse ran out the door [fingers or mouse run away],
Hickory dickory dock.

Taking this further

If it is still fun, try a couple or all of these (don't forget the chimes):

The clock struck five/The mouse took a dive

The clock struck six/The mouse went in two ticks

The clock struck seven/The mouse went to heaven

The clock struck eight/The mouse didn't wait

The clock struck nine/The mouse did whine

The clock struck ten/The mouse came down again

IDEA 14

The Old One-Two

EYFS Aspect	Resources	Group Size
Numbers as Labels and for Counting	None	1–3 children

Another old favourite action rhyme:

One, two, buckle my shoe [mimic shoe tying]

Three, four, knock at the door [knock four times on table or floor]

Five, six, play some tricks [hide face behind hands and say 'boo' as you take them away]

Seven, eight, stand up straight [sit or stand up straight]

Nine, ten, sit down again [flop down on the floor].

Taking this further

If it's still fun, go on to 20:

11, 12, reach the shelves [both hands high in the air]

13, 14, buttons need sortin' [fiddle with buttons]

15, 16, do some fixin' [mime hammering, fist onto hand]

17, 18, tired of waitin' [mime sleeping]

19, 20, that seems plenty! [open both hands].

IDEA 15

Who's Eaten the Buns?

EYFS Aspect	Resources	Group Size
Numbers as Labels and for Counting	Five cherry-topped buns – could be cut-out pictures from a cake box, play dough, etc.	1–5 children

This is the old favourite, *Five Currant Buns*.

Lay out the representations of the buns. Count them with the children.

Do the actions as you say the rhyme:

> Five currant buns in the baker's shop [indicate the buns],
> Round and fat with a cherry on the top [move arms in a wide circle, touch hand to head],
> Along came [child's name] with some money one day [child mimes giving money if possible],
> Bought a currant bun and took it away [child takes bun or is given it].

Verse two/three/four/five

> Four/Three/Two/One currant buns . . . [if more than one child, change customer's name each time].

Verse six

> No currant buns in the baker's shop [outstretched open hands],
> Round and fat with a cherry on the top [repeat actions of previous verses],
> Along came [adult's name] with some money one day,
> But there were no currant buns to take away [say last line sadly and make sad face].

To round off, count each child's buns with them to see who has the most, remembering the adult has none!

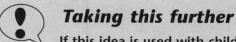

Taking this further

If this idea is used with children in the older age groups then you could start with any number of buns. Also, the children could take more than one bun in any given verse, e.g.:

Ten currant buns . . .

Along came [name] with . . .

Bought *two* buns and took them away.

Eight currant buns . . .

The counting backwards would be very tricky for this!

IDEA 16

Adventurous Ducks

EYFS Aspect	Resources	Group Size
Numbers as Labels and for Counting	Six plastic ducks or six separate duck pictures (five ducklings and one mother duck) Blue sheet or model pond optional	1–5 children

Count the ducks and explain the family of five ducklings and the mother who has to make sure they are all safe.

Tell the rhyme:

Five little ducks went swimming one day [move five ducks over the pond],
Across the pond and far away [put one duck aside],
Mother Duck said, 'Quack, Quack, Quack, Quack' [wiggle Mother Duck],
But only four little ducks came swimming back [bring four back].

Verse two/three/four

Four/Three/Two little ducks . . .

Verse five

One little duck went swimming one day,
Across the pond and far away,
Mother Duck said, 'Quack, Quack, Quack, Quack',
And FIVE little ducks came swimming back!

Taking this further

Allocate children to manipulate the ducks.

Two Little . . . Allsorts

EYFS Aspect	Resources	Group Size
Numbers as Labels and for Counting	A number of pairs of objects/ finger puppets	1–3 children

This is the *Two Little Dickie Birds* rhyme which can be extended to so many things which can disappear and reappear:

● Start with the birds:

Two little dickie birds, sitting on the wall [wiggle index fingers, clad in a finger puppet if possible]
One named Peter [wiggle left finger]
One named Paul [wiggle right finger]
Fly away Peter [put left hand behind back]
Fly away Paul [put right hand behind back]
Come back Peter [return wiggling left finger]
Come back Paul [return wiggling right finger].

● Use other characters – remember to include appropriate actions:

Two little teddies, sitting on the table
One named Georgie, One named Mabel
Run away Georgie, Run away Mabel
Come back Georgie, Come back Mabel.

Or:

Kittens lying on the bed/Sooty/Jed/Run away/Come back
Children sitting down to play/Rosie/Faye/Jump up/Sit down
Children sitting on a chair/Thomas/Claire/Jump up/Sit down
Children standing very still/Zander/Bill/Run around/Come back

Taking this further

If making your own rhymes to the names of the children taking part, start with the second child's name, e.g. Hannah. Then think of an action for the two, e.g. 'waving a big banner'. One or other of two names will be easier of course but it is also likely that none rhyme easily!

Shifting Sands

EYFS Aspect	Resources	Group Size
Shape, Space and Measures	The sand tray and a range of containers of different shapes and sizes, e.g. plastic jugs, small and large yoghurt pots, cuboid plastic containers	1–3 children

When the children are playing in the sand tray they need time to explore independently and free play is important. However, there are ideal opportunities to structure part of the play into thoughts about measuring and space.

● Encourage the children to experiment with transferring sand between containers of differing shapes and sizes.

● Talk about containers being 'full, half full' or 'nearly full' and so on.

● Talk about which is 'heavy, heavier and heaviest'.

● Pose questions like, 'Can we put some more sand in this one?'

Taking this further

Similar opportunities arise out of water play but it is probably best not to do both sand and water at the same time.

Safety Note

Use unbreakable equipment.

Measure Me

EYFS Aspect	Resources	Group Size
Shape, Space and Measures	Tape measure Record book (optional)	Individual

This activity could start at any age and continue, periodically or at quite regular intervals, to chart growth. Most children are thrilled to know they are growing and love to be involved with their measurements but a few may feel uncomfortable. Choose carefully what is to be measured (see below) in order to avoid embarrassment and make sure the child is happy.

Recording can be as elaborate and formal or simple and informal as you like. It can be included with any system of records which includes the child's interests and other details. It can be put in a book, 'About Me', with the child's artwork, or it can simply be taken in isolation as a point of interest on that particular day.

- However the information is to be used, make sure the child is involved throughout.

- Talk about what measurements are going to be taken and about growing in general.

- Show the tape measure and explain how it is used, pointing out the numbers you are going to read. Of course, the numbers will not mean much to the child at all at this stage but the familiarity will grow.

- Suggested measurements: height (perhaps easiest measured with child lying down); arm length; head circumference; foot; hand span.

- If the adult is measured as well, then more vocabulary can be introduced, e.g. 'bigger than', 'shorter than', 'growing up'.

Taking this further
As confidence with physical activity grows, length of stride could be measured and even timing completion of an obstacle course.

Section 3: 16–26 months

With a growing confidence in walking, this is the age for counting out steps on short special distances or while being aided up or down a few stairs. Language development is rapid too so the children will want to repeat the names of numbers and shapes. Don't forget that most of the ideas included in the previous two sections can and should be used with this age group.

Who Lives Here?

EYFS Aspect	Resources	Group Size
Numbers as Labels and for Counting	Up to five cardboard boxes with openings which look like a door Soft toys for each house Paint and brushes	1–4

The idea of this game is to present the concept of house numbers. The children can be involved with painting the boxes or not depending on how much mess can be allowed.

● Paint the boxes to look like houses ensuring the openings look like a door.

● On each box write a large number, 1–5, depending on how many boxes are being used.

● Set the boxes out in a row as in a street, terrace-wise or with spaces between.

● There are endless possibilities to include gardens, a road, traffic, shops and a park depending upon how far you wish to take it.

● Once everything is set up, choose soft toys or toy figures to live in each house, using the children to help decide who lives where. It is important to emphasize the house numbers in this process: 'Let's have Mrs Bear in Number three', placing Mrs Bear in the box with three on it, closing the door and pointing out the number.

● When all the toys are 'at home' you can begin some little scenarios.

● Involve the children in discussion on what each is doing: 'Bingo is sitting at home at Number three watching the television,' and so on.

● The scenarios then become more elaborate as various characters come out from their numbered house to go to the park or tidy the garden or to visit neighbours (remembering to quote the house numbers each time).

● Involve the children as much as possible with the invention of the little stories revolving around everyday activities, always remembering to put in a plug for the house numbers whenever it seems appropriate without upsetting the flow of the game.

● End the game by asking the children who lives where as they all return 'home' from wherever they are in the story. Can they remember and put them back in the right house?

The boxes can be flattened after the game and stored ready to be reused another time.

Taking this further

For this idea, numbers do not necessarily have to be consecutive although it consolidates counting if they are. Older children may wish to use their own house numbers and they can be expected to take on more responsibility for the story-telling. In fact they may well demand it!

Bus Ride

EYFS Aspect	Resources	Group Size
Numbers as Labels and for Counting Calculating	Chairs or cushions Soft toys	1–4

This is all about an imaginary bus ride and thinking about the numbers of passengers getting on and off:

- Set up an imaginary bus using several chairs or cushions.

- The children and adult take a seat on the bus each and any number of soft toy friends can take other seats.

- Everyone needs to be seated comfortably at the start with everyone paying for their ticket as they get on. This is an opportunity to emphasize vocabulary like 'behind', 'beside', 'in front of'.

- As the bus sets off – with appropriate sound effects – the game takes the children on a bus journey and the imagination can go wild with the things seen on the way. Passengers get on or off at the bus stops, e.g. 'Jack got off to have a ride on Thomas the Tank Engine'/'Maisie got on and sat behind Bob the Builder'.

- At various points, the number of passengers left on the bus can be counted or actual sums calculated, e.g. 'Becky and Monkey got off at the park to play on the swings which left one, two, three, four, five passengers on the bus' or 'Jack got back on the bus on his way home which made one, two, three, four, five, six to go on to the next stop'.

- The amount of times the adult actually counts the passengers or the complexity of the calculations depends entirely upon the interest of the children. A good test for whether or not the child is up for counting is if he/she is happy to join in at some level. If not, it is probably best not to bother and just enjoy the ride with all its imaginary comings and goings: there is always another day.

- It would be very appropriate to finish this game with the song, 'The Wheels on the Bus', perhaps making up new words referring to the passengers used in the play.

Taking this further

The children could pay for their tickets with plastic or card coins. The driver can give change occasionally. Older children could be expected to give a 'correct' number of coins, e.g. the driver asks for a number between one and five and that amount has to be given.

Tea Time

EYFS Aspect	Resources	Group Size
All	Cups, saucers, plates, etc. and play kitchen paraphernalia	1–4

Have a make-believe tea party for soft toys or the children themselves. Include lots of discussion about the numbers involved, for example:

- If we have four cups, how many saucers will we need?
- Count out the different items for 'one each' either as actual numbers or 'one for you, one for Jack, one for Jaz'.
- Involve the children in deciding if there are 'enough' of the various items.
- Talk about the shapes and sizes of the various tableware items.

Taking this further

Older children can be expected to respond more numerically and actually count out the items. If play dough or similar material is used as play-food this is a great opportunity to discuss equal portions and dividing up.

Safety Note

None if the usual kitchen play equipment is used.

Sort the Shape

EYFS Aspect	Resources	Group Size
Shape Space and Measures	A wide range of different 2D or 3D objects which are either square, round or triangular	1–4
	Three nominated toy characters to receive them (optional)	

This is a sorting activity for shape.

● Spread out the objects randomly and talk about them, picking out the more interesting ones, pointing out the edges and other characteristics.

● Explain that 'pig' is in a round mood today and wants all the round shapes – 'giraffe' is in a triangular mood and wants all the triangles – 'Ted' wants to load all the square shapes into his lorry.

● Ask the children to give the right shapes to the right toy.

Note: All the children can sort all the shapes at the same time or each shape can be allocated to an individual, swapping over the allocation for a second or third game.

Taking this further

Older children can think about the differences between square, rectangle, cube and cuboid (box), circle, sphere (ball) and cylinder (tube), but the basic shape names are sufficient for this stage.

Safety Note

Avoid sharp, heavy or very small objects.

The Long and Short of It

EYFS Aspect	Resources	Group Size
Shape, Space and Measures	Balls of wool Glue, paint & paper (optional)	1–4

This idea allows practice in the vocabulary of 'long/longer/longest' and 'short/shorter/shortest' (in the linear sense rather than time). Although it can be a fun game simply to loosely tangle and then untangle the woollen threads, it is far more interesting to use the various lengths in making a collage.

Option 1:

● Paint a sheet of paper, about A4, in any way the child chooses. Colours should contrast to the colours of the wool which will be used for collage.

● While the paint is drying, cut wool in varying lengths. Involve the child(ren) in discussion as you lay out the lengths.

● Talk about the colours of course but, essentially, the lengths. 'Which is the longest/shortest?'

● If the interest is there, you could try placing a few in length order.

● Eventually the discussion centres upon how the strands can be arranged on the painted background to make a picture or pattern and the work on this can be completed.

Option 2 (without the paint and glue):

● Choose contrasting colours of wool and cut various lengths; thicker ply is best for this.

● Tangle them very loosely in a sort of maze. You could set the scene by blaming the muddle on Teddy or someone and ask for help to sort out his mess.

● Ask the child(ren) to 'pull out a long blue one' or ask 'can you find a short green one?'

● When all the threads have been separated, ask, 'which is the longest/shortest?' and then make Teddy put them all away tidily.

Taking this further

Option 1

Areas of the artwork can be made up of either the short strands or long strands, e.g. 'We need some long straight wool for the path' and 'We need some short pieces for the tree branches'.

Over, Under, Round, Through

EYFS Aspect	Resources	Group Size
Shape, Space & Measures	Obstacles such as cushions and 'arches', blankets, large hoops	1–4

This idea builds the vocabulary of position. The enjoyment value is the 'assault course'. It can be played indoors or out and does not need much space:

● Set up an 'assault course' in the available space of a room and have the children (adults too if you like) go through it.

● Here is the vocabulary to present and some ideas of obstacles which can be used, in any order of course:

Over the rocks – large cushion/s

Under the dragon's wings – small blanket laid on the floor

Round the tree – solid object to go round once, twice or any number of times without dizziness

Through the cave entrance – a large plastic hoop

Up the cliff – onto a soft chair or beanbag

Down to the ground – from the soft chair or beanbag

Across the crocodile river – scrunched-up blanket.

Taking this further

There could be treasure at the end of the course perhaps in the form of a cardboard medal with a shiny sticker on it.

Safety Note

Going too fast or more than one child at a time could result in crashes. It should not be a race. Beware carpet burns!

Slotting Shapes

EYFS Aspect	Resources	Group Size
Shape, Space & Measures	Shallow cartons of different shapes, e.g. triangular (there is a certain chocolate assortment packaged in this shape), square, rectangle, round, oval Pieces of card cut either to fit exactly or same shape but smaller paints or colours (optional)	1–4

This is a home-made shape-matching game:

● If you choose to include a little artwork, the children can paint or colour the shapes – or some of them – in whatever way they wish.

● Spread the shapes across the table or floor at random (you could blame teddy for the muddle).

● Pick up examples of the shapes and talk about them.

● Ask the children to place the shapes in the right boxes.

Taking this further
Count the numbers of each shape with the children.

Building Understanding

EYFS Aspect	Resources	Group Size
Numbers as Labels and for Counting Calculating Shape, Space & Measures	Set of wooden or plastic interlocking building bricks	1–3

- Give the children lots of bricks leaving only a few for yourself.

- Ask, 'Who's got most?'

- Discuss with the child or group, using vocabulary: 'same, lots, few, more than, less than, fair, share, big pile, smaller pile'.

- Share out: 'one for David, one for Jasmine, one for me, one for David, one for . . .' and so on until all bricks are equal.

- Play a game of building towers. Who can build the tallest, thinnest? Who can make the longest line of bricks?

Taking this further

Start off with one big pile of bricks. Have child divide it into two piles he/she considers to be equal. Then count bricks or build towers to check the estimate.

IDEA
28

Sort 'em Out

EYFS Aspect	Resources	Group Size
Numbers as Labels and for Counting Calculating Shape, Space & Measures	Set of coloured bricks or plain with coloured spots drawn or stuck on	1–3

- Together, sort the different colour bricks into piles.

- With the children, estimate which is the biggest/smallest pile or if they about the same.

- Build a tower together with, say, all the blue bricks, then yellow, followed by all the other individual colours available.

- Ask the questions: 'Which tower is smallest/tallest/highest/shortest?' 'Are any towers the same size?'

Taking this further

Race to build the tallest tower in 1 minute or while counting slowly to 10. Who was first/second/last?

Which tower is taller/shorter?

Which fell down first?

Can we make a taller tower in the same time?

Treasure Hunt

EYFS Aspect	Resources	Group Size
Shape, Space & Measures	Selection of safe, simply-shaped items Prepared cards with simple shape on each, e.g. circle, square, line, thin shape – to match the items	1–3

- Each child either chooses or is given a card.

- Discuss the shapes, using the vocabulary, e.g. 'round/long, thin/square/triangle/tube.

- Children go off to find an item matching the shape on their card, e.g. a ball for the circle, a straw for the long, thin shape, a plastic brick for the square.

- Alternatively two cards can be made for each shape and the children find the matching card rather than an item. This would be easier but not so much fun.

Taking this further

Use more complex shapes on cards and have children find a matching card OR cut-out shape.

Ready, Teddy, Go

EYFS Aspect	Resources	Group Size
Numbers as Labels and for Counting Calculating	Three cards each with either one or two or three spots Three teddies or cuddly toys Three hats/scarves (for teddies) Three teaspoons Three yoghurt pots	1–3

- Set the scene, 'Some teddies are going out for tea and we need to help them.' Then go through the stages, supporting the counting and vocabulary as you go.

- First, the child picks a card to find out how many teddies are going by counting the spots.

- Child gets that number of teddies ready with hat and scarf for each.

- Travel with the teddies to wherever the tea party is to take place, e.g. at the table/behind the sofa.

- Make sure each teddy has a teaspoon and yoghurt pot plus any other items chosen for the 'meal'.

Taking this further

Child can help find all sets of three, counting into piles as they go.

Does it Fit?

EYFS Aspect	Resources	Group Size
Shape, Space & Measures	Empty grocery box with one small, one larger square hole cut in one side Variety of safe toys and/or household objects to post through	1–3

- Children love to 'post' things. The object of this activity is to help them estimate shape and size. The children simply try to post all the chosen items through one or other of the holes.

- Talk about the various objects you have chosen for posting, including the shape, feel and size.

- Encourage the children to think first if a given object might go in the small hole, rather than putting everything, even the smallest items, in the large one. Ask which might go in the large hole but not the small one. Ask if any objects are too big to go in either of the holes.

- As well as items which easily fit, try to include some which can be fed in carefully one way but not another or something which might be squashed or squeezed in.

Taking this further

Explore the idea that the box has capacity for lots of small things but only a few big things.

Items can be described by the adult to indicate which one to pick up, e.g. that little teddy/the bigger teddy with the blue waistcoat/the long wooden spoon.

Everything in the Kitchen Sink

EYFS Aspect	Resources	Group Size
Shape, Space & Measures	Sturdy chair (if using a kitchen sink) Towels on floor and on child Clean sink with clean cold water Plastic jug Plastic mugs with handles Plastic bowl Teaspoon	Individual

- Set the scene for 'helping in the kitchen'.

- Using the sink of water, ask the child to decant various quantities for you using the vessels, e.g. 'Can you give me a jug of water to fill the kettle/fill a saucepan for potatoes/fill the bowl to wash windows?'

- For smaller quantities which need to be more carefully measured out, ask for 'three teaspoonfuls', 'three more', 'three more' and so on until there is enough to mix up, say, the gravy powder.

- Use the vocabulary: enough/not enough/more/too much/a little less. Help and encourage the child to successfully make the right quantities.

 Taking this further

Ask child which vessels would be best to transfer water from the sink for a particular amount or purpose.

Safety Note

Make sure the child knows the difference between cold and hot water, and that the sink may be a safe place to play but the cooker is not.

Runner Beans, Jumping Beans

EYFS Aspect	Resources	Group Size
Numbers as Labels and for Counting	The child	Any

This short activity can be part of a movement session, either as a warm-up or a warm-down.

- Adult calls out 'runner beans' and children run on the spot.

- Adult calls 'jumping beans' and children stop and wait for either 'one' or 'two' or 'three' to be called.

- Children jump that number of times on the spot, counting the jumps together.

- The game can end with the call, 'baked beans', which means the children lie down flat on the floor.

Taking this further

Jump and count any appropriate number up to 10 but keep to mostly lower numbers to avoid tiring.

Safety Note

Ensure there is ample space all around each child.

Don't let children throw themselves down after jumping as they do in musical bumps.

Section 4:
22–36 months

As children reach three years their idea of number is becoming fixed. They make valuable comparisons between much of what they see around them. This allows them to sort and categorize objects and ideas. Remember that most of the activities included in the previous three sections can be used with this age group.

Supermarket Shapes

EYFS Aspect	Resources	Group Size
Numbers as Labels and for Counting Calculating Shape, Space & Measures	As many clean empty cartons, small plastic containers, yoghurt pots as possible Chunky plastic play coins or paper money	1–4

- Set up a shopping game.

- Either the adult or one of the children can be on the checkout, with or without a till.

- Children select and buy items – the amounts do not need to be accurate, although older children may be able to count out a small number of coins.

- At some point, introduce the shapes of the sides of the items – ask individuals to buy only the *'square'/'round'/'long, thin'* shapes.

- Talk about the various items and their packages, emphasizing shape as well as appeal.

Taking this further

Specify the number of items to buy or count the number of items in the shopping.

Safety Note

Caution: Danger of swallowing or pocketing the play coins.

Use chunky plastic discs or paper money for under 3 years.

IDEA 35

Spot My Number

EYFS Aspect	Resources	Group Size
Numbers as Labels and for Counting	Large simple pictures of ladybirds, butterflies and other insects essentially with different total numbers of spots, 1, 2, 3, 4, 5 on the wings or body Number cards 1, 2, 3, 4, 5	1–4

This activity seeks to clarify the relationship between numerals and quantities, in this case, spots.

- Talk generally about butterflies, ladybirds and other insects.

- Show the picture cards and talk about the colourful wings and bodies, pointing out the spots.

- Ask the children to place the number cards with the corresponding spots for each creature.

- You could finish with some artwork where the children make a picture of, say, a four-spotted insect.

Taking this further

Increase the range of numbers.

Use pictures containing different numbers of similar objects, e.g. three people at a bus stop or four bicycles.

Five in the Bed

EYFS Aspect	Resources	Group Size
Numbers as Labels and for Counting Calculating	Something soft on the floor as a 'bed'	1–5

An old favourite nursery rhyme so useful for counting backwards and early ideas of subtraction.

- Set out a large 'bed' on the floor and set the scene by lying down to sleep on it.

- Have all the children lying side by side and start the rhyme with the number of children, say 'five'.

- Say the rhyme:

  There were five in the bed and the little one said, 'Roll over, Roll over',

  So they all rolled over and one fell out and banged his head and gave a shout.

  [End child rolls out but DOES NOT bang his/her head!]

- Continue counting down in the rhyme, losing one child at a time, until there is just one left:

  There was one in the bed and the little one said, 'That's good, now I can have the bed all to myself!'

Taking this further

When the children ask to do it again they can take it in turns to be the 'Little One'.

Throw in a mathematical challenge: 'How many would be left if two fell out?'

Doctor, Doctor!

EYFS Aspect	Resources	Group Size
Numbers as Labels and for Counting	Any play equipment for doctors and nurses	1–4

- Set up a role-play doctors' surgery or clinic, or join in the play at a convenient moment.

- An adult takes on the role of doctor or nurse or helps a nominated child carry out an 'examination' of the patients.

- Count various body parts and check they are in working order, e.g.:

  - *One, two arms* [wave the arms about, one at a time]

  - *One head* [gently nod the head to and fro]

  - *One, two, three, four, five fingers* [tweak them as they are counted – NB If it is a child taking the role of the nurse, the numbers do not necessarily have to be right or in order]

  - *One, two ears* [whisper in each ear].

- Any non-taboo body part can be counted with its associated check for function, including the heart with a play stethoscope and appropriate sound effects. Hairs on the head may be a little too far though!

Taking this further

The fingers/toes count can be used as a check on counting ability at a later age.

Safety Note

Need to be sensitive to the individual child's feelings about his/her body generally and any physical disability in particular.

Three Little Pigs

EYFS Aspect	Resources	Group Size
Numbers as Labels and for Counting Calculating Shape, Space and Measures	A copy of *The Three Little Pigs* story (depending upon questions)	Any

This and the following activity, *The Billy Goats Gruff,* are examples of how a story reader can ad lib during the story to both engage the listener and emphasize the number content.

● Settle down to read the story.

● Remember that the enjoyment of the story is the most important part of the activity and over-questioning on the numbers could spoil it.

● Include, with pauses for discussion and ad lib on characters and situations, some questions and statements on the numbers involved, e.g.:

  – How many pigs have escaped now? (If it is a version where they run to the next pig's house.)

  – How many pigs have been eaten now? (If it is a version where the pigs are eaten by the wolf.)

  – How many apples do you think the third little pig picked from Farmer Smith's orchard?

  – The wolf went higher and higher and higher until he reached the chimney.

  – How did such a big wolf fit into the chimney?

  – Emphasize the timings when the pig tricks the wolf by arriving early for each meeting.

Taking this further

Toys to represent the characters can be animated during the telling of the story. This will also enable the children to see more easily the numbers involved at various stages. CAUTION: Some children may be sensitive to realistic acting.

Billy Goats Gruff

EYFS Aspect	Resources	Group Size
Numbers as Labels and for Counting Calculating Shape, Space & Measures	A copy of *The Billy Goats Gruff* story (depending upon questions)	Any

This and the previous activity, *The Three Little Pigs*, are examples of how a story reader can ad lib during the story to both engage the listener and emphasize the number content.

● Settle down to read the story.

● Remember that the enjoyment of the story is the most important part of the activity and over-questioning on the numbers could spoil it.

● Include, with pauses for discussion and ad lib on characters and situations, some questions and statements on the numbers involved, e.g.:

– How many goats are left waiting to go over (after Little Billy Goat Gruff goes over the bridge)?

– Emphasize the relative sizes of the goats: little, middle-sized, great big.

– How many are enjoying the green grass now?

> ### Taking this further
> Similar treatment can be given to other number stories, like *Goldilocks and the Three Bears* or, indeed, any story where things can be counted in the illustrations.

Taking Turns

EYFS Aspect	Resources	Group Size
Numbers as Labels and for Counting	Large cloth bag Set of numbered cards, 1/1st, 2/2nd up to the number of children	1–4

This can be used for deciding the order of participation in any significant activity.

● Choose an activity all the children want to do but which requires taking turns, e.g. riding around a course on a tricycle.

● Each child takes a card from the bag.

● Make sure they all know the place they have picked and they are ready in that order. Emphasize the connection between one and first, two and second and so on.

● Set the children on the course in turn according to the order.

● When all turns are taken it can be repeated with a different selected order.

 Taking this further

This method of choosing an order can of course be used with many different events and activities.

IDEA

41

Teddy Bear Sports Day

EYFS Aspect	Resources	Group Size
Numbers as Labels and for Counting Shape, Space & Measures	Silver cups or medals made from foil, one per toy entrant Cushions, and other 'obstacles' Teddies or soft toys as athletes	1–3

● Make a simple obstacle course for the teddy athletes: cushions to climb over, chair to climb onto, kitchen roll tubes to jump over.

● Adult and/or children manipulate the toys on the obstacle course – one at a time – to jump over, run along, climb up, crawl under and balance.

● Commentate on the way to increase the excitement and include the vocabulary, 'along/under/over/through/up/down/around/across'.

● Hold an award ceremony at the end. Discuss with the children how many cups/medals are needed so that each teddy receives one and check with them if there are enough trophies.

● Award one trophy to each toy after deciding 'first, second, third'.

● End with rousing cheers and clapping.

Taking this further

Ask children to commentate on their teddy's race or describe, after the obstacle race, some or all of what their teddy did.

IDEA 42

Spot the Ones and Twos

EYFS Aspect	Resources	Group Size
Numbers as Labels and for Counting	The environment	1 or 2

This activity is ideal for developing observation as well as number recognition and awareness.

● When on an outing or short walk, look out for objects in single units, e.g. one policeman/one bus/a single dog, cat or bird/the number one written on a sign.

● At a convenient point change the rule to find twos, e.g. two people together/ two ducks/two wheels on a bike/the number two written on a sign.

● Remember to include this only as an addition to the general pointing out of interesting sights and events on the outing.

● On return, together with all the other reminiscences, ask a few questions like: 'How many buses did we see?', 'How many swans were on the lake?'

Taking this further

Discuss and investigate how numbers are used on signs, shops, doors and car number plates in the environment.

Safety Note

The usual safety rules for out-and-about apply here.

IDEA 43

What's the Time, Mrs Smith?

EYFS Aspect	Resources	Group Size
Numbers as Labels and for Counting	None needed unless the game follows a wolf story, e.g. *The Three Little Pigs* or *Little Red Riding Hood*	1–4

This is the traditional game with a simple variation to avoid frightening the children.

NB The traditional game, using a 'wolf' and 'dinner time' can be quite disturbing for the imagination of small children so it is recommended that the wolf is changed to 'Mrs Smith' and the final time to 'bath time'. However, if you are using the original wolf of the game then you might read a wolf story where the creature is shown as scary but easily tricked.

- The adult takes the part of 'Mrs Smith', at least in the first instance, and walks randomly around the space – either indoors or out – followed by the children.

- The children chant, 'What's the time, Mrs Smith?'

- In response, 'Mrs Smith' calls a time, say, '2 o'clock' to which the children clap twice.

- Being safe, the group moves on and the children soon repeat their chant. Different times answered need the correct number of claps.

- At some point, Mrs Smith answers 'Bath Time!' which is the cue for the children to escape and Mrs Smith to chase, catching (but not bathing) one of the children.

 Taking this further

Increase the range of times called.

Safety Note

Usual care with a chasing game.

Edible Calculations

EYFS Aspect	Resources	Group Size
Numbers as Labels and for Counting Calculating	Snack with up to five pieces, e.g. apple or banana slices, orange segments, dried fruit	1–4

Used occasionally, this activity may make snack time a little more interesting.

● Join in with the snack.

● Count the components of the snack together.

● As each one is eaten count what's gone and how many are left.

Taking this further

Make double identical quantities.

Count the items.

Child shares: 'one for me, one for you'.

Eat items in unison.

Count items gone and remaining over the two plates.

Safety Note

Hand hygiene.

Emphasize that child is helping to prepare the snack, not 'playing with food'.

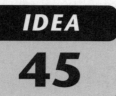

Musical Show Me

EYFS Aspect	Resources	Group Size
Numbers as Labels and for Counting	Music that's easy to stop/start or singing voice (nothing too fast or loud)	Any

Follow the style of musical statues.

- Play some favourite recorded music which invites gentle swaying movement rather than fast and frenetic.

- Children warm up with any movement they wish, after being told to stop when the music stops.

- After a minute or so, stop the music.

- Call a number and body part, say 'show me two knees'.

- The children indicate the appropriate body part or object, in this case by covering both knees.

- Quickly check everyone has the right answer before restarting the music for the next round, say, 'show me one hand'.

- Numbers greater than one or two can be called if you say, for example, 'show me four fingers' prompting the child to hold up or cover the correct number.

Taking this further

Extending the instruction when the music stops to activities will increase the numerical possibilities, e.g. 'clap four times'/'turn around twice/three times'/'jump five times'.

Safety Note

Care when moving around – turn slowly.

Fetch!

EYFS Aspect	Resources	Group Size
Numbers as Labels and for Counting	Child-safe items or own toys in box or positioned around room Empty toy box or cardboard box	1–4

This activity can be used as part of a real tidying-up operation if toys are spread around naturally or as a staged tidy-up.

- After a general play session with all the selected toys and games, and with the usual warning that the play is about to end, explain that help is needed to tidy up by putting things in the toy box in the right order.

- Give each child a specific task associated with numbers, e.g. 'please put two books/three cars/four skittles in the box'.

- It is far more simple if everything is to go into a single box, of course, but it can include more positional vocabulary with, e.g., 'please put three books onto the shelf' or 'please put the giant teddy and two small teddies on the cushions'.

Taking this further

Count the items, target 10, altogether in the box.

Many opportunities here for vocabulary and understanding that the quantity changes as things are added or taken away.

Drinking Game

EYFS Aspect	Resources	Group Size
Calculating Shape, Space & Measures	Plastic see-through cups or beakers (all the same) Jug which the children can use safely Drinking water Straws (optional)	Small

As there could be some water spillage, this should be done on towels or a waterproof surface.

● Help the children fill the cups and compare amounts so that they are the same quantity.

● Take turns to drink a small amount and compare the levels again. Drinking straws will make this more manageable.

● Use the vocabulary: more/less/lots/not so much/a little bit more/same/equal/enough.

● Finish by drinking up the water.

Taking this further

Try to drink the right amount to more or less match the level in another beaker which is left undrunk as a model to copy.

Sorted for Spoons

EYFS Aspect	Resources	Group Size
Shape, Space & Measures	Selection of different-sized spoons: tea- dessert- table-spoons Selection of different-sized plates or bowls *Goldilocks and the Three Bears* story	1–4

- Read the story of *Goldilocks and the Three Bears.*

- Show the jumble of spoons and set the task to sort them into three piles: one for Baby Bear, one for Mummy Bear and one for Daddy Bear, i.e. little/small, medium/middle-sized, big/large.

- For interest and discussion you could include a fourth category of cooking spoons, e.g. a wooden spoon or ladle, ensuring, of course, they are not necessarily allocated to Mummy Bear's set.

- Similarly sort the plates or bowls for each bear.

- Finish with a child taking the part of Goldilocks and miming the porridge-tasting, using the appropriate spoons and bowls.

Taking this further
The whole story could be acted/mimed with four children.

Going Up, Going Down

EYFS Aspect	Resources	Group Size
Numbers as Labels and for Counting Shape, Space & Measures	Toys based on graduated sizes e.g. stacking rings or cups/ Russian-dolls-style nestling toys/ 4/5 different-sized balls, tennis through to football-sized	1–3

● Begin by playing with the stacking or graduated toys.

● Move on to placing them out in random order and ask the children to help organize them in order of size, smallest to largest.

● Spread them out randomly again before asking for them to be arranged largest to smallest.

● Each time, count the items in the set.

Taking this further

If you would like to add an element of challenge then, when the child is familiar with the items in a given set, secretly remove one and ask in which position the missing one belongs. The 'discovery' of the missing object could be found in the counting process. ('Oh dear, one's missing, which one is it?')

IDEA
50

Round as Saucers

EYFS Aspect	Resources	Group Size
Shape, Space & Measures	Picture books or store catalogue	1–2

Add an element of shape identification to sharing a book.

- Settle down to look at and talk about a picture book or store catalogue, one with plenty of quite detailed pictures.

- As well as talking about what is going on in the pictures, suggest the child looks for round shapes on the pages and cheers (quietly) when one is seen. Accept anything that looks elliptical (squashed circle) as the child may realize that it is round in real life.

- Consolidate by drawing a circle in the air with the child each time one is found.

- Remember that the circle shapes could be part of a bigger picture, e.g. chimney on top of a house.

Taking this further

Progress to triangles and squares, being prepared to introduce 'rectangle' or 'oblong' as a long sort of square with two longer sides.

IDEA

51

One, Two, Number My Shoe

EYFS Aspect	Resources	Group Size
Numbers as Labels and for Counting	Household objects including clothes Lots of cards with one, two or three on them as numerals AND as spots	1–4

● Set out objects in their groups, e.g. one jumper, two shoes, three bricks.

● Challenge the children to place the number/spot cards to the correct group, giving support as necessary and to maintain interest.

● Finish with some little scenarios, e.g. 'One teddy said to three bricks, "Shall we build a tower?"' or 'Two shoes walked to one pushchair and sat by it'.

Taking this further

Increase the range and numbers and spots up to 10 on the cards.

Section 5:
30–50 months

Now the children are older and more able to talk about the pictures in books it is worth remembering numbers while sharing them. As well as talking about what is happening in a picture, many illustrations will lend themselves to counting, e.g. 'How many animals can you see? Let's count them'. Remember that most of the activities included in the previous four sections can be used with this age group.

Make a Story

EYFS Aspect	Resources	Group Size
Numbers as Labels and for Counting Calculating	Available 'props' and visual aids	3–6 children is ideal but it works well with more

With the children in a group, make up a story involving numbers and calculations. The individual children are the 'characters' involved with whatever props are available. The more drama, animation and involvement of the children the better. Here is an example:

Five children: Jessica, Elisha, Thomas, Ezra & Tyne.

One adult: Bernice.

Resources: chimp hand puppet; bag with five pine cones.

One day, Jessica, Elisha, Thomas, Ezra and Tyne went into the garden to play. There were [count the group] six altogether. Ezra sat on the bench with Bernice and they read a book. Jessica and Thomas played on the swing. Elisha rode around on the tricycle and Tyne drove along in the car. [Each acts a little mime for the games they play.] After a while, Elisha noticed a little chimp [produce hand puppet] hiding in a bush. Elisha called the others and they gathered around very excited, wondering what the chimp was doing there.

The chimp was very shy but they encouraged him out and then saw he was holding a little bag. Bernice sat the chimp on her lap [animate chimp] and he whispered in Bernice's ear. He told her that his name was Barney and there were magic pine cones in the bag which could grant wishes. If you shake the pine cone and whisper your wish into Barney's ear your wish could come true. Not always – and never straight away – but it could if you wished hard enough. Each pine cone could be used only once and then it would disappear.

The children wondered how many pine cones there were. Would there be enough for each of them? Bernice emptied the bag and out came what seemed like ordinary pine cones. Could they really be magic? Everyone counted them. 1-2-3-4-5. Was that enough? [Go through to match cones to children] One missing! But Bernice said she had a wish come true last week so she didn't need another one today.

The children took it in turns to try out the magic. First, Jessica chose a pine cone and thought very hard. She shook it gently, gave it to Barney and whispered her secret wish into his ear. The pine cone disappeared. [Adult gives appropriate reaction with Barney and hides cone.] Will it work? Nobody knows.

Now, how many cones were left? [Count the remaining four.] Then Ezra chose a pine cone. [The process is repeated for all children until all the cones are used – remember to question how many are left and count each time. A good idea is to recap the order the children wished to emphasize first, second, third, fourth and fifth or 'last'.]

When all the wishing had been done, Tyne asked Bernice what she would have wished for if she had the chance. Bernice thought for a while and then said, "I think I'd have wished that Barney could stay with us all the time." And that is what happened. Barney moved in with everybody and they played with him every day.

Taking this further

Artwork: 'Barney' (or the central character of a different story) and the correct number of 'cones' (or other items used in a different story).

IDEA

53

Making Picture Pairs

EYFS Aspect	Resources	Group Size
Numbers as Labels and for Counting	Pictures of individuals or pairs stuck onto cards for matching (ideas list below) Magazines and store catalogues are a good source for the pictures	1–4

● Begin by explaining what pairs are, i.e. two things which belong together rather than simply two items.

● Show the picture cards and talk about them.

● Set the challenge to match the pairs.

Ideas for pairs:

arms   curtains   earrings   ears   elbows   eyes   feet   gloves   hands
knees   legs   shoes   skates   wellies   wings   (aeroplane and bird)

Taking this further

•   Try concentrating on a single type of pair, e.g. shoes, using a wide range of different styles of footwear.

• Get into the animal world with pairs of animal legs/feet/eyes/ears.

• Clarify for the child, 'a pair of trousers' (each leg is a trouser) – similarly a pair of sunglasses, scissors.

IDEA
54

Collage Shapes

EYFS Aspect	Resources	Group Size
Shape, Space & Measures	Gummed or self-adhesive shapes of different sizes and colours Paper of different colours	1–4

This is an artwork activity with just a few shape rules.

● Spread the gummed shapes out on a table.

● Set the challenge to make a picture using only the gummed shapes, e.g. people playing with a ball.

● The paper chosen will set the background colour.

Taking this further

• Set the challenge to make a picture (or pattern) using only one type of shape, e.g. circles. Anything can be drawn to add to the circles, e.g. a tree trunk added to a green circle.

• Divide a sheet of paper into four sections so that a pattern can be made in each section for different shapes: squares, circles, triangles, stars.

IDEA 55

Spot the Difference

EYFS Aspect	Resources	Group Size
Numbers as Labels and for Counting Calculating	Photocopied sheets – see below Colours or paints	1–4

Butterflies are used as an example here because they are particularly colourful animals but any creature could be used, e.g. ladybirds or the three-legged spotted gumblegrig.

● Make photocopied pictures of line-drawn butterflies with spots. There should be four or five identical animals on each sheet EXCEPT that one must have ONE fewer spots than the others, e.g. three with four spots and just one with three spots.

● Talk to the children about the possible colours they could use to make them really colourful.

● Before they start the artwork, ask them to spot the difference with the spots, counting with them as necessary.

● After marking in the missing spot, the children complete the pictures.

Taking this further

• **Increase the number of spots from which one is missing, e.g. three with six spots and one with five.**

• **Make the difference in number of legs rather than spots.**

IDEA 56

Where's the Number?

EYFS Aspect	Resources	Group Size
Numbers as Labels and for Counting	Set of magnetic numbers and letters Fridge magnets (optional) Magnetic surface	1–4

- Talk to the children about using the magnetic letters and numbers. Include fridge magnets if you wish, for added fun and interest.

- Let the children play with the magnets, forming whatever patterns or arrangement they wish.

- At some point jumble the letters and numbers together and ask the children to find the numbers. Remember '0' and 'O' and '1' and 'I' can be confused.

- Set the task of separating the numbers from the letters.

Taking this further

Ask the children to place the numbers in sequence.

Safety Note

Any fridge magnets must be child safe.

IDEA 57

One Man Went to Mow

EYFS Aspect	Resources	Group Size
Numbers as Labels and for Counting Calculating	Toy dog Toy lawn mower or push-along toy	1–5

This is a sing-a-long activity with the old nursery favourite. A carpet indoors can be 'mowed' just as effectively as a dry lawn.

- Choose one of the group to be the man with the dog and start the song:

  One man went to mow, Went to mow a meadow,

  One man and his dog [woof!]*, Went to mow a meadow* [child and dog push the mower around the space].

- Add child two for the next verse:

  Two men went to mow, Went to mow a meadow [both go round with the mower],

  Two men [child two jumps], *one man* [child one jumps] *and his dog* [woof!]*, Went to mow a meadow.*

- Add a new child for each verse until everyone is used up. Remember, they jump as their number is counted down.

- The last verse, say for five men, is:

  Five men went to mow, Went to mow a meadow [all five plus dog and mower go round],

  Five men, four men, three men, two men, one man and his dog, Went and mowed a meadow. And now the job's all done! [all sit down together]

IDEA
58

How Many Wriggly Rattlesnakes?

EYFS Aspect	Resources	Group Size
Shape, Space & Measures	Pictures of snakes (optional)	1–4

- Talk about snakes and, in particular, their movement.

- Ask the children to move around the floor like snakes, sound effects are good.

- Choose an appropriate time to ask for the:

  longest snake [children stretch out arms];

  shortest snake [children put arms to sides];

  fattest snake [children make a star shape];

  thinnest snake [children turn onto sides];

  bendiest snake [children curl round];

  noisiest snake [children hiss].

- Instructions can be repeated in different order.

Taking this further

Set a task to collectively make the longest snake possible. Try it in a straight line, bendy and coiled.

Safety Note

- When making the joined snake it is best to join hand-to-hand and foot-to-foot to avoid kicks to the head.

- Beware carpet burns.

IDEA 59

The Enormous Turnip

EYFS Aspect	Resources	Group Size
Numbers as Labels and for Counting Calculating Shape, Space & Measures	Copy of *The Enormous Turnip* Turnip (optional) Toys to represent the characters (optional)	1–5

This is another opportunity to use a story time to emphasize the vocabulary of number and shape.

● Settle down to read the story, *The Enormous Turnip*, with, perhaps, a short discussion on growing vegetables and showing a real turnip.

● You could use appropriate toys to represent each character as they are called upon to help.

● Pause after each character is brought in to ask, 'How many are pulling the turnip now?' and help to count.

● Reiterate with each addition to the tugging line that the characters are getting smaller. Use the vocabulary through discussion and questions:

'big/bigger/biggest'; 'strong/stronger/strongest'; 'small/smaller/smallest'; 'weak/weaker/weakest', together with the synonyms: 'tiny/little/small' or 'huge/big/large/massive'.

The 12 Days of Christmas

EYFS Aspect	Resources	Group Size
Numbers as Labels and for Counting	Props for the song (optional)	Any

● The full 12 days may be too many for younger children so you may want to shorten it. 'Five gold rings' is a logical cut-off point.

● Here are some alternative – hopefully easier – lines to use with the same tune:

> On the first day of Christmas my true love gave to me, a fairy for the Christmas tree
>
> . . . second day . . . two shiny stars and a fairy for the Christmas tree
>
> . . . third day . . . three silver balls, two shiny stars and a fairy for the Christmas tree
>
> . . . fourth day . . . four chocolate coins, three silver balls, two shiny stars and a fairy for the Christmas tree
>
> . . . fifth day . . . five go..old rings! four chocolate coins, three silver balls, two shiny stars and a fairy for the Christmas tree.

● If you want to go further:

> . . . sixth day . . . six Santas singing
>
> . . . seventh day . . . seven reindeer running
>
> . . . eighth day . . . eight sleigh bells ringing
>
> . . . ninth day . . . nine crackers snapping
>
> . . . tenth day . . . ten snowmen melting
>
> . . . eleventh day . . . 11 lanterns swinging
>
> . . . twelfth day . . . 12 candles glowing

Step in Time

EYFS Aspect	Resources	Group Size
Numbers as Labels and for Counting Shape, Space & Measures	Movement music and player	Safe for the space

This activity needs to be repeated a number of times before children become used to the instructions and shapes to make.

- Begin with a familiar warm-up activity.

- Choose a simple tune which is not too fast.

- Children move freely to the music in the available space.

- Call instructions as they move, e.g. 'big/huge/giant steps'; 'small/little/tiny steps'.

- After a reasonable time, stop the music and have the children lie on the floor and relax.

- Call instructions: 'make yourself huge/tiny, [children spread out/curl up on floor]

  'make a one' [children either stand to attention or lay flat out]

  'make a two' [children kneel and drop head forward].

- Finish with a repeat of the musical steps.

Safety Note

Usual precautions for a movement activity.

Cinderella

EYFS Aspect	Resources	Group Size
Numbers as Labels and for Counting Calculating	Any available props to do with the story and its characters	Any

An activity for Christmas/pantomime time.

Settle down to tell the story of *Cinderella.* Here is a brief outline with suggestions for bringing out the number content:

● Cinders with stepmother and ugly sisters – doing all the work – invitations to the Ball – Cinders has too much work and is too ragged.

● Fairy Godmother arrives – new dress – coach from a pumpkin.

● White horses from six white mice [gather and count six mice – can be extended by collecting, say four, and asking, 'How many more do we need?'].

● Footmen from two toy soldiers [again, gather soldiers in any way, e.g. 'We have four so how many do we take away to leave the two?'].

● Fairy Godmother's warning on time to return [talk about the clock].

● Cinders goes to the Ball – dances with Prince.

● Clock strikes 12 [do the chimes as a group].

● Cinders rushes out, leaving glass slipper.

● Prince's search reveals all [try obviously wrongly-sized dressing-up shoes on some children].

● Cinders and Prince live happily ever after.

Taking this further

Try giving other pantomime stories the same number treatment, e.g. *Jack and the Beanstalk*.

IDEA
63

Touchy-Feely Numbers

EYFS Aspect	Resources	Group Size
Numbers as Labels and for Counting	30 cm lengths of fluffy knitting wool 30 cm lengths of smooth twine Fine glass paper cut into 15 cm high number 1's A4 card Washable PVA glue or similar Art materials and artshirts	1–4

This is an arty activity centred around making and recognizing numbers.

● Preparation:

  – Draw faint, 15 cm high numbers on the cards, some '1', some '2' and some '3'.

  – Make some 15 cm high '1' numerals from fine glass paper.

● Talk about the shapes of numbers 1, 2 and 3. In particular, show that the number 3 goes in at the centre and goes back on itself before the final outward curve.

● Help the children to make the numbers on the A4 card.

  – For 'No. 1' stick the glass paper within the lines.
  – For 'No. 2' stick a fluffy wool length over the pre-drawn number.
  – For 'No. 3' stick a twine length over the pre-drawn number.
  – More than one length can be used for the 2s and 3s to increase the thickness if the child does not obscure the shape.

● Allow the children to decorate their numbers artistically.

Taking this further

Include Nos. 4 and 5, using, e.g. fur fabric strips for '4' and salt dough or play dough for '5'.

Safety Note

Ensure hands are washed well after using the glue.

I-Spy Sets

EYFS Aspect	Resources	Group Size
Numbers as Labels and for Counting Calculating	Two sets of three objects e.g. cups, pencils Two sets of two objects Two different single objects e.g. one teddy, a favourite ball	1–4

This is a variation of the traditional I-Spy-With-My-Little-Eye game.

- Set out the sets of objects, e.g. three cups, three pencils, two bricks, two cars, one teddy, one ball.

- Explain that the twos and threes are in 'sets' or groups that like to stay together and today the single items want to be on their own.

- You could count the items in each set with the children if you wish, depending upon the amount of support you feel they need.

- Explain that you are looking at a set and the game is for the children to guess which one it is.

- Say, 'I spy with my little eye a set of three. What could it be?'

- In this example the response of 'cups' or 'pencils' would win and with the praise you count the threes with the children to be sure.

- Similarly, say, 'I spy with my little eye a set of two. What could it be?' Follow up in the same way when either of the correct responses is given.

- For the single items say, 'I spy with my little eye just one something beginning with [initial sound of one of the objects].'

- Continue the game dotting about between singles, twos and threes.

Taking this further

- **Children take turns to set the question with 'I spy . . .' while adult and other children guess.**

- Increase the numbers in sets if confident of success.

IDEA 65

1,2,3, Which Number Can You See?

EYFS Aspect	Resources	Group Size
Numbers as Labels and for Counting	Four cards numbered with a large '1' Four cards numbered with a large '2' Four cards numbered with a large '3' NOT spots, this game is numeral recognition	1,2,3,4 or 6 (to divide equally into 12)

- The children could have the opportunity to decorate the cards before the game as long as the numerals remain very clear.

- Jumble up the cards.

- Children take turns to set them out on the floor, helping them say the number as they lay each card.

- Ask them in turn to find the number 1, 2 or 3 until all cards are gone, e.g. 'Aysha, please find us a number 2'. The children do not have to find equal numbers of ones, twos and threes but try to ensure they each have at least one of each number to hold.

- When all the cards are taken, count how many cards each child has. They should all have the same number if you have been careful to be fair.

- Play the game as many times as they can, and a slight variation could be with a nominated child in turn asking a friend to pick a particular number.

Taking this further

- Increase the number range if the children are secure with recognition of 1, 2 and 3.

- Ask the children to arrange the cards in numerical order.

Snap!

EYFS Aspect	Resources	Group Size
Numbers as Labels and for Counting Calculating	The following or similar: Ten bricks Ten toy cars Ten crayons	1–4

- Set out the objects in separated, single piles.

- One child picks up some of the objects from one of the piles, e.g. three crayons (he/she can pick up any number up to five, leaving five or more for the second child to choose from).

- The second child must pick up the same number of the same object without counting them out, i.e. an estimate.

- Talk about the two piles: 'Do we think the piles are the same/different?' 'Which has more/less?'

- Children count first, then call 'Snap!' if they think it is the same number.

- Check with the children that a call is right or wrong.

Useful vocabulary: one more/one less/not enough/not so many/too many/ about the same/same.

Taking this further

Children take turns to hold up 1–5 fingers. Others take turns to 'grab' that number of items as quickly as possible.

Guesstimating: A Teddy Bear Picnic

EYFS Aspect	Resources	Group Size
Numbers as Labels and for Counting Calculating	4–8 teddies or dolls according to the number available and to ability of child or group to count up to eight Coloured bricks as pretend food Teaspoons (About twice as many bricks and spoons as there are teddies)	1–4

- Choose a particular colour of brick to represent food, e.g. yellow = piece of cheese/red = strawberry/green = apple.

- If natural wood bricks are used, choose different shapes, e.g. rectangle or square = piece of cheese/cylindrical brick = chocolate roll.

- Seat the teddies for a 'meal'.

- Ask the children to guess or 'estimate' how many of each 'food' will be needed for each teddy or doll to have one each. Put the estimated pile to one side.

- Do the same with the spoons.

- When all estimates are complete and the piles are ready they can be shared out, one for each toy.

- Discuss the results: 'Are there enough/spares/too many?'

- Discuss which estimates were about right. Praise all estimates, even if wildly inaccurate.

- Repeat activity to ensure success with more guidance if necessary.

- Finish with an imaginary teddy bears' picnic including songs and games.

Safety Note

Some children of this age may still like to put things in their mouths. Emphasize this food is only pretend.

IDEA
68

It's a Gift

EYFS Aspect	Resources	Group Size
Shape, Space & Measures	Wrapping paper Familiar objects to wrap	1–4

This activity could be part of a wider celebration for a 'birthday' for Big Ted.

- Preparation:

  - Choose about 4–6 familiar objects with clearly-defined shapes – e.g. book, toy car, ball – and wrap them in bright paper.

- Gather round Big Ted or whatever cuddly toy is chosen to have a birthday and sing *Happy Birthday*.

- Show the wrapped presents and talk about what might be inside them, highlighting the guesses which involve deduction through shape, size and weight.

- Take each shape in turn and establish what is thought to be inside.

- Help Big Ted to open and reveal correct or incorrect result.

- Finish by either helping Big Ted play with the presents or playing party games.

Taking this further

Place one or two 'presents' in a box so that the item itself is not defined in any way. Describe its identity as clues little-by-little until the children have guessed correctly or close and reveal.

IDEA

69

It's the Same!

EYFS Aspect	Resources	Group Size
Numbers as Labels and for Counting Calculating	Giant sponge die Six different sets of familiar child-safe objects	1–4

- Sit with the children in a large circle.

- Place six sets of objects in the middle, e.g. one teddy, two books, three skittles, four bricks, five cars, six large counters. Make sure the groups are clearly separated and children can see the individual components of each set.

- Count the number in each set with the children.

- Roll the die and count the number of spots. Ask which group of objects has the same number in it as the number of spots on the die.

- Children then take it in turns to roll the die.

- Everyone in the group tries to be the first to come up with the answer each time.

Safety Note

Beware tiny objects that could be swallowed.

Circles that You Find

EYFS Aspect	Resources	Group Size
Shape, Space & Measures	16 cards with a shape drawn on them: Four with a circle Four with a rectangle Four with a triangle Four with a star	1–4

This is a treasure hunt game.

● Decide on an area for the hunt. This could be in one room or more, even a whole house, depending upon the degree of safe movement which can be afforded to the children.

● Without the children seeing, place three of each card around the chosen area, where possible against, under or on objects of the respective shapes.

● Show the children the fourth set of cards and talk about all the shapes. Discuss the shapes of things in the room, e.g. a round clock, square seat, rectangular box.

● Allocate one child to each shape and explain that three similar cards are hidden in the chosen area. The game is for them to find their shape only and leave any other cards for the others to find.

● When all cards have been found, decide who the 'winners' were, ensuring they all won for some reason:

  – The one who searched most carefully instead of just looking randomly

  – The one who found all his/hers first

  – The one who was calmest

  – The one who tried hardest.

Safety Note

It is not a race. Keep it calm, especially if it is up and down stairs. Make sure hidden cards are in easily accessible places.

IDEA 71

Wind the Bobbin Up

EYFS Aspect	Resources	Group Size
Shape, Space & Measures	The child	Any

The traditional song and tune: *Wind the Bobbin Up.*

● Sing the song with the children, teaching the actions:

> *Wind the Bobbin Up, Wind the Bobbin Up [roll hands around each other],*
>
> *Pull, pull, clap, clap, clap [pull elbows downwards, then clap three times].*

Repeat these two lines.

> *Draw a big circle [draw circle in air with one hand],*
>
> *Draw a big square [draw square in air with one hand, starting in top corner],*
>
> *Point up here, point down there [point to ceiling, then to floor],*
>
> *Clap your hands together, one, two, three [clap one, two, three],*
>
> *Rest your head and go to sleep [lay head on folded hands – snore gently].*

Wait for a few seconds then wake them up unexpectedly with:

> *Wind the bobbin up . . . [repeating the whole song once more].*

Taking this further

Children may like to take turns to stand either individually or in pairs next to the adult and 'lead' the song.

Safety Note

Make sure there is space for elbows to fly about during 'pull, pull'.

IDEA 72

Why Did You Put it There?

EYFS Aspect	Resources	Group Size
Numbers as Labels and for Counting Shape, Space & Measures	Set of coloured bricks or any collection of child-safe objects that can be sorted in terms of colour and/or shape, size, 'got wheels', 'got two/four legs' (animals set) according to ability	1–4

This is a sorting activity which can be as closed or open-ended as you wish.

● Spread out the chosen objects and talk about the attributes with the children.

● Help children sort the objects into sets according to similar attributes, for example:

- set of yellow/ red/blue bricks
- set of bricks with only straight sides
- set of bricks with curves
- set of animals with four legs
- set of animals with two legs.

● Encourage children to explain why they have chosen a particular category, i.e. 'I put them together because . . .'

Taking this further

- Some children will notice that some things overlap two categories, e.g. a set of animals that are black and have four or two legs could be sub-divided into sets of black with two legs and brown with four legs.

- Draw large circles on several sheets of paper and add simple line drawings to denote a set, e.g. an oval with head on four sticks = animal with four legs. Children then put the appropriate animals into the circles on the sheets of paper to make correct sets.

Assume the Position

EYFS Aspect	Resources	Group Size
Shape, Space & Measures	Cuddly toy or favourite toy car	1 or 2

This activity is to help develop positional vocabulary.

- One child takes the cuddly toy for a walk or the car for a drive around the room.

- After visiting lots of places, ask the child to leave it somewhere for a while. For this example we will have Harry finishing with his toy car under a chair.

- Ask questions that require the child to choose between two possible answers. In this example: 'Has Harry parked his car beside the chair or under the chair?'

- If the child is unsure or answers wrongly, ask him/her to put his/her hand on the car and ask, 'Is Harry's hand on the chair or under the chair?', etc.

- Always help the child to success, praise and reiterate the correct answer.

- The child, or the second child, takes the teddy for a walk or car for a drive again, leaving it somewhere else ready for more positional questions.

- Allow plenty of opportunity for the child to chat imaginatively about where the teddy or car is going and what it is going to do. The positional questioning should be incidental as far as possible.

Possible vocabulary pairings:

in/outside, over/under, above/below, under/beside, close to/far from, on top of/underneath, beside/on top of

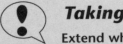

Taking this further

Extend what the teddy or toy does on its journey, e.g. jumps over, wriggles like a worm under, stands upside down on the table, vrooms through the tunnel.

Shall I Be Mother?

EYFS Aspect	Resources	Group Size
Calculating Shape, Space & Measures	2–3 teddies/soft toys/dolls in ascending sizes Plastic beakers or cups in three clearly different sizes Jug or plastic teapot Drinking water	1–4

- Discuss how adults and children in the same family may have different sized meals and drinks, e.g. Dad has five fish fingers, children have three/Dad has a big mug of tea, children have a small beaker of juice.

- Set the scene with the teddies wanting a drink after a lot of exercise.

- Ask the children to place the teddies in order of size and match the three beakers to them.

- Help the children to pour water into each beaker to about 3 cm from the top.

- Talk about the sizes and quantities.

  Possible vocabulary: bigger than, biggest, smaller than, smallest, enough, not enough; the biggest teddy must have the biggest/most drink.

- Finish with helping the teddies to drink up the water before taking them off for more exercise.

Taking this further

- Use play dough to create the different-sized meals on three different-sized plates.

- Use same-size cups but put differing amounts in for different-sized people/teddies.

IDEA 75

Wake Up! Wake Up!

EYFS Aspect	Resources	Group Size
Numbers as Labels and for Counting Calculating	The children Different colour beaker for each child	Small

- Children curl up as though asleep.

- Choose a child and ask for his/her favourite colour. Let's say the answer is 'red'. Child lies down again.

- Say the following rhyme with children joining in when they know it:

    Mum made a cold drink in a [red] *cup*
    Couldn't find [name of chosen child] *to drink it all up*
    She went upstairs and then she saw
    [child's name] *curled up asleep on the floor*

    Children shout quietly:

    Wake Up! Wake Up, [child's name]!

- [Child] stands/sits next to the adult and mimes drinking from his/her cup.

- Ask, 'How many children are awake?' and 'How many are still asleep?'

- The first child chooses the colour of cup for the next child and the rhyme is repeated using the new colour and name and asking the same resulting number questions.

- Keep the verses going until all the children are awake. Ensure that 'zero' is emphasized as well as 'nobody'.

 Taking this further

Make a similar rhyme to go in reverse order, sending the children back to sleep one by one:

Mum made a cold drink in a [red] cup,
[Child's name] was too tired to drink it all up.
So he went upstairs and curled up tight,
Go to sleep [Child's name] Say goodnight.
        [Child] whispers 'Goodnight'.

Section 6:
40–60+ months

Children at this age develop logical thinking. The richness of the experiences they have already encountered combine with sophisticated language and social skills to enable them to solve problems. Remember that most of the activities included in the previous five sections can be used with this age group.

IDEA 76

Play Dough Maths

EYFS Aspect	Resources	Group Size
Numbers as Labels and for Counting Calculating	Play dough (bought or home-made)	1–4

This can be part of a wider play-dough food-making session.

- Make 5–10 items of a single type of food from play dough, e.g. sausages OR peas. The exact number depends upon children's ability.

- Divide the food into two piles, e.g. four peas and two peas.

- Ask children how many altogether and count with them.

- If necessary, show children how to count the four and count on.

- Note that some children may say 'One, two, three, four,' then 'One, two' for the second group so they will need to be helped to understand that in order to find how many altogether they will need to keep counting from the first total.

- If appropriate, reverse, i.e. pile of two then four to show the same answer.

- Let children put out peas in two piles and 'test' you to reinforce.

- If children are confident, try putting all the peas together, count them, remove some, say two, and see how many are left.

- Ensure everyone manages at least one sum by counting independently – even if it is two and one to three – so they experience success.

- When the maths is over, make more types of play dough food, serve up on paper plates and enjoy the meal.

Taking this further

- **TIP: Mime putting one pile (the larger one) in pocket and count on to the second pile, e.g. 'four in pocket, five, six, seven'.**

- **Put out three different numbered groups only two of which add to a required amount. Help children to choose the two groups which make the number, e.g. put out groups of four, three and two. Ask which two groups make five and/or which two groups make seven.**

- **If a child is ready to understand you can use statements like, 'four and three make seven altogether'.**

IDEA 77

Stand in Line

EYFS Aspect	Resources	Group Size
Numbers as Labels and for Counting Calculating	Children	Up to 10 or 12

When children need to line up, e.g. to wash hands, or at drink or fruit time, try leaving a little extra time for this number activity.

Ask:

- 'How many children are standing at the door ready to wash hands?' Prompt the answer '0' or 'zero'.

- 'If your name is [Jake] go and be first in line at the door.'

- 'How many at the door now?' Answer, one.

- 'If one more stands at the door, how many is that?'

- 'If you have [red shoes*] go and stand behind [Jake].'

- 'How many are ready in the line now?'

- 'How many will there be when the next person stands behind [last child's name]?'

  - * Ensure that each name/attribute (Jake/red shoes) refers only to one child so you can add one at a time to the line.

- Continue to prompt children in line as well as those waiting to say how many are in the line and what the next number will be each time, up to 12, according to numbers involved and ability. They may need reminding not to leave themselves out when counting.

 Taking this further

- Vary the way children walk to the line, e.g. tiny steps/ sideways/slow motion.

- Add on two children at a time – e.g. Two Stephens/Two with a yellow top.

IDEA

78

Follow the Die

EYFS Aspect	Resources	Group Size
Numbers as Labels and for Counting	Giant sponge die	Any

- Sit with the children in a large circle.

- Roll the die into the middle and check everyone knows how to recognize the spots representing a certain number.

- Children take it in turns to roll the die into the middle. Everyone holds up the same number of fingers as shown on the die as soon as they can.

- When everyone has had their throw, start another round but this time they clap the correct number of times. NB It will be wise to wait at each throw for everyone to work out the number (supporting as necessary) and then give a signal to clap together.

- Repeat with fingers and claps if interest is still there.

Taking this further

For a larger group, have everyone spread out in a room or garden area. When the die is thrown the children make groups of the number shown on the die. The inevitable ones left over get to throw the die for the next go.

Kim's Game

EYFS Aspect	Resources	Group Size
Numbers as Labels and for Counting Calculating Shape, Space & Measures	Set of about six familiar small objects (too big to swallow) Set of about six plastic or card shapes Set of about six plastic numbers, e.g. magnetic Tray and cloth cover	1–4

- Arrange about six familiar objects on a tray, e.g. toy car, pencil, crayon, multilink brick, item of doll's clothing, jigsaw piece.

- Cover with a cloth.

- Explain to the children that they will have a little while to look at and remember what is on the tray before one item is removed and they then have to say what has been taken, taking it in turns to have a go.

- Remove the cloth and show the items to the first child. Talk about the items to support memory.

- Briefly take away the tray and secretly remove one of the items.

- Ask the child what is missing, giving support as necessary.

- Repeat the game using six shapes, e.g. square, circle, star, triangle, semi-circle, pentagon. Expect children to draw shapes like pentagon and semi-circle in the air if they cannot remember the names.

- Repeat the game using six numbers (1–6).

Taking this further

Play Kim's Game with card or plastic coins.

Safety Note

Beware small objects.

IDEA 80

Football Crazy!

EYFS Aspect	Resources	Group Size
Numbers as Labels and for Counting Calculating	Giant paper clips or toy clothes pegs String Paper Scissors (adult use only) Art materials (not paint)	1–4

● Preparation:

  – Cut out eleven identical football shirts from paper; about A5 size. Write numbers 1–11 on them.

  – Cut out eleven identical pairs of shorts in proportion and write the numbers on them also.

● Talk to the children about football and include how the shorts and shirts get very dirty. Explain that it is washday and the kit has to be hung out to dry.

● Show the 'kit' that you have cut out, explaining that there are 11 players, one of which is the goalie. Count the shirts and then the shorts to match.

● This is an opportunity to secretly remove shorts or shirts in whatever quantities you feel matches the abilities of the children in order to set a problem or two, for example:

  – 11 shirts spread out with nine shorts arranged under them. 'How many more pairs of shorts do we need?'

  – Seven complete sets of kit spread out. 'How many players have not put their kit in the wash?'

● Agree on colours for the strip, e.g. red shirts, black shorts, and ask the children to colour them. The goalie shirt, Number 1, should be multicoloured. This will be the 'washing process', i.e. returning the clothes to the original colour.

● Suspend some string as a washing line in a convenient place. Have the giant paper clips (44) ready as pegs.

- When all are coloured, they need to be hung out to dry. First, help the children match the shirt numbers with the shorts.

- More number problems can be included in the discussion over pegs and how many are needed for each item of clothing, e.g. 'How many pegs do we need for three shirts?' or 'I have eight pegs, how many pairs of shorts can I hang with them?'

- Peg out the washing in order of shirt numbers.

- When all is done make sure the kit is all there ready for the next match by counting together.

Taking this further

Number problems you devise can be as complex as you wish within the abilities of the children.

IDEA

81

Holiday Time!

EYFS Aspect	Resources	Group Size
Numbers as Labels and for Counting Calculating	A wide range of familiar objects Suitcase	1–4

This is an innovative story session.

- Preparation:
  - Make sure you know up to ten different small or medium-sized things around you, most of which can come in numbers up to ten.

- Sit the children in a group and explain that you are going on holiday. You can make up any destination (or it could be fact) and the things you hope to do.

- Bring your fantasy to a close by explaining that you have to pack and go through the packing list in order (all of the following are suggestions only):

  - One iron because my clothes will be creased in the suitcase

  - Two books to read on the beach

  - Three jumpers in case it gets cold

  - Four cuddly toys to keep me company

  - Five toy cars for [Ted] to play with

  - Six postcards to send to friends ... and so on up to ten (actual objects are best, of course, but representational objects can also be used with a bit of imagination).

- Each set of items should be collected and counted in the middle of the group as they are called for, with nominated children gathering them as appropriate.

- When everything is there, ask a few challenging questions like, 'How many more books would I need for each cuddly toy to have one?'

Taking this further

A nominated child could list his/her packing in the same way, with help from the adult and the rest of the group.

IDEA 82

What's the Shape?

EYFS Aspect	Resources	Group Size
Shape, Space & Measures	Pictures of toys and familiar objects Copied silhouettes of pictures (see below)	1–4

- To prepare:
  - Find 6–10 pictures of familiar objects and toys in magazines and store catalogues which have a clear outline of the item.
  - Cut them out carefully around the actual outline.
  - Turn them over and black out the entire shape. (You will need the picture itself.)
  - Arrange them, black side up, on a photocopier and make two or three copies.
  - Save the pictures for setting the puzzle.
- Show the set of pictures (right way up) and talk about them, including some details about the shapes.
- Show the silhouettes (shadows) and ask if anyone can spot what they are.
- Finish by finding one or two of the items represented in the pictures and playing with them if appropriate.

(!) *Taking this further*

If you have access to an overhead projector (OHP), you can make silhouettes of the children's heads. Shine it on to a large piece of paper fixed to a flat wall. A child stands against the paper facing sideways and you draw around the shadow.

Safety Note

An OHP is reasonably safe for this but any light source with a more direct beam of light can be damaging to the eyes if the lamp is looked at directly.

IDEA 83

Halves and Quarters

EYFS Aspect	Resources	Group Size
Calculating Shape, Space & Measures	Large coloured circles and squares Glue sticks if shapes are not gummed Paper (for sticking the shapes onto)	1–4

● Preparation:

  – For this activity all the circles must be the same size and all the squares must be the same size.

● Cut some of the circles and squares into halves and quarters.

  – Cut just one quarter from some of each of several shapes.

● Talk to the children about the full-size circles and squares. Explain how you have made the half and quarter shapes.

● Ask the children to make full-size circles and squares from the pieces you have cut by sticking them together onto paper. There is no need to match the colour, in fact it is more effective and artistic if they are different.

 Taking this further

  • The preliminary discussion could include halves and quarters of an apple or other fruit which could be shared when you have finished with the demonstration.

  • Cut out magazine pictures of faces (essentially full face). Cut them in half and ask the children to match the two sides. NB It is more of a challenge to match halves when they are cut horizontally. It may also be interesting to try faces cut into quarters!

  • If you want to combine faces in this way 'wrongly' it can be a lot of fun but they need to be more or less the same size. The internet is a good source of same-size faces.

Two-by-Two (Noah's Ark)

EYFS Aspect	Resources	Group Size
Numbers as Labels and for Counting Calculating	Lots of animals in pairs, preferably one male, one female, e.g. bull and cow, lion and lioness An ark or something to represent it, e.g. a box *Noah's Ark* story	1–4

- Tell or read the story of Noah's Ark.

- Show and talk about the animals.

- Decide together which animals are going in the Ark and in which order.

- Put them in 'two-by-two' to appropriate parts of the Ark, i.e. 'rooms' where they will be safe from the dangerous ones!

- As much as possible without losing the interest in the activity, involve the children in counting the groups as they build up and change.

- Typical discussion points:

  - Shall we put the [cows] with the [sheep]? How many animals would that be altogether?

  - We've got three kinds of animals in that corner. How many is that?

  - How many would we have left in that corner if we took the [lions] away from the [goats]?

  - How many animals have we got altogether? (No need to count them all in this situation but estimates could be interesting.)

- Finish with a general play with the animals.

Colour by Numbers – 1

EYFS Aspect	Resources	Group Size
Numbers as Labels and for Counting Calculating	Colouring book with simple line drawings Art materials	1–4

- Preparation:

  - Choose a page from a colouring book which has a picture with large areas to colour; one page per child.

  - Write numbers in the areas so that they can be clearly seen but which will be covered by the child's colouring, ideally about five different colour areas.

  - Separately, draw large numbers, one to however many areas there are to colour, and against each make a patch of whatever colour would be appropriate for the respective numbered areas. If you have made the same colour choices for each child's picture then you will need only the one 'key' chart.

- Give the pictures for the children to colour, explaining the need to match the colours to the numbers.

Taking this further

Use more elaborate pictures with greater range of numbers/colours. Help children to make their own key.

IDEA 86

Colour by Numbers – 2

EYFS Aspect	Resources	Group Size
Numbers as Labels and for Counting	Stiff card Pages from a colouring book Art materials Glue stick	1–4

- Preparation:

  - Cut four pages from a colouring book, preferably the kind which is printed on one side only.

  - Use a template to cut out the same-size shape from each page. The shape will be easier to fit back in place accurately if it is not a circle. All shapes must be the same but they can be cut from different parts of the respective pictures.

  - Stick the pictures, minus cut-outs, to stiff card.

  - In the spaces left by the cut-out, write the numbers one to four

  - On the back of each of the cut out shapes, write the corresponding numbers to their matching picture. Double check that you have the right numbers for the right pictures!

- Show the pictures to the children and explain that there is a puzzle to do before colouring. They have to match the pieces to the right pictures first . . . and without seeing the drawing on the missing shape.

- Point out the numbers on both picture and upturned shapes and ask the children to match the numbers.

- When all shapes are matched, stick them in the spaces and let the children choose which picture to colour.

> ## Taking this further
>
> - **Cut more than one identical shape from each picture and increase the range of number-matching.**
>
> - **To develop shape recognition, make all the cut-out pieces a square but draw different shapes on each and the corresponding spaces.**

The Snake Pit

EYFS Aspect	Resources	Group Size
Shape, Space & Measures	Paper Scissors (adult use only) Play dough Wax crayons	1–4

- Preparation:

  – Draw and cut out several snakes of different lengths and different degrees of bends in the bodies; some quite curled and others more like a winding lane.

- Talk to the children about snakes generally.

- Ask them to make snakes of their own with the play dough. You may need to assist with uniformity of body and if you want the heads to be realistic.

- When there are several snakes finished (the children can make more than one) show them all together and ask for them to be placed in order of length. They will need to be carefully straightened for this. You could also order them according to fatness/thinness.

- Show your paper snakes and discuss which are the longest/shortest, allowing for the extra difficulty of the bendy shapes which cannot be straightened.

- Ask the children to estimate which of their play-dough snakes would fit on top of the paper snakes and test by moulding the chosen ones on the paper partners.

- The children can then change the lengths of their play-dough snakes by making them fatter or thinner to fit onto the paper ones. When doing this they will have to do a great deal of trial and error which is very valuable. The discussion involved in assisting them is also very necessary.

- To finish, the children could colour your paper snakes.

Taking this further

Cut lengths of string or wool, some of which are the exact length of some or all of the paper snakes. Ask children to estimate which string is the same length as a snake.

IDEA
88

Drawing Numbers

EYFS Aspect	Resources	Group Size
Numbers as Labels and for Counting	Printed sheets as below Rubber stamps pictures (optional) Art materials	1–4

● Preparation:

  – Divide an A4 sheet of paper into five sections, graduating in size.

  – Choose a theme, e.g. animals (preferably a theme for which you have a set of rubber-stamp pictures).

  – Stamp one [animal] in the smallest section, two (not necessarily the same as the first but should be the same as each other) in the next sized section, three in the third and so on to five in the largest section.

  – The object of the activity is for the children to write the corresponding number with each animal group. Some children will need the support of dots or some other device to help them make the numbers correctly. If so, this should be added at this stage.

  – Make copies of the sheet for the number of children.

● Talk to the children about the pictures and how they could be coloured.

● Count the animals in each section with them.

● Set the task to colour the pictures and add the correct numbers in each section. Encourage the children to make more than one of each number in the respective sections for practices.

Taking this further

- Make a second sheet for the numbers 6–10.

- Some children may like to make their own number picture by choosing one number, say '4', writing that number and drawing the correct number of similar objects.

Tea Time – The Real Snack

EYFS Aspect	Resources	Group Size
Numbers as Labels and for Counting Calculating	Normal snack time requirements	1 or 2

Why not use one or two of the children to help with refreshment time?

- Talk to the children about laying the table for a snack. Discuss what drinks and food there will be and what is needed for them, e.g. plastic cups, plates, spoons.

- Count the children who will be sitting at the table, using fingers: Charlie, one; Rosie, two; Darryl, three; and so on. If there are too many at one table then it will have to be restricted to a smaller, perhaps friendship, group.

- Once the number of diners is established, ask how many cups, plates, etc., will be needed. Have the children count them out as they place them.

- When a number of smaller food items need to be shared so that each child has more than one, try working out the division sum with the diners. How many apple segments are there? How many of us are there? Are there enough? How many will each have? Will I get one?

- Occasionally there may be a large cake to share which needs cutting. This can be an ideal opportunity for a larger group discussion on how many pieces are needed. And we surely could not miss such an opportunity to talk about equal-sized, smaller, smallest, bigger and biggest pieces!

Safety Note

Normal precautions should be taken when small children are helping to lay the table. Plastic or paper ware is advisable. Cutting implements should be kept out of reach of the children.

Match the Die

EYFS Aspect	Resources	Group Size
Numbers as Labels and for Counting Calculating	Giant sponge die Large blank playing cards Large counters or tokens (optional)	1–4

This game can be played for rewards, e.g. tokens exchangeable for stickers or special privileges.

● Preparation:

– Write the numbers 1–6 on the blank playing cards, one set for each child.

– Make a second group of sets with tally marks instead of numerals.

– Make a third group of sets with a chosen shape, say stars, instead of numerals.

NB – You may not wish to use all of these sets every time.

- Sit with the children in a large circle on the floor.

- Show the die and numbered card set and explain how the spots on the die correspond to the numerals, giving examples.

- Explain the rules of the game:

    - Everyone lays their set of cards out face up in front of them.

    - Children take it in turns to roll the die.

    - Everyone has to hold up the card with the number that matches the spots as soon as possible, with great cheers when it is achieved.

    Tokens/counters can be awarded either to the first to show the correct number or to anyone that manages to do so, however much they are supported. It is important, of course, that they all receive a good number of tokens if they are being awarded.

- Play the game with as many rounds as you wish.

- If the children are enjoying the game, repeat with tally marks and/or stars, after explaining the differences.

Taking this further

Add a challenge of 'add one to' or 'take one from' the die spots shown. This would mean increasing the numbered cards to zero–seven.

Safety Note

Ensure that the tokens or counters are too large to be swallowed.

IDEA
91

Mr Square/ Mrs Round

EYFS Aspect	Resources	Group Size
Shape, Space & Measures	Art materials Examples of shapes Different sizes of stick-on shapes (optional)	1–4

- Talk about shapes and show examples. Point out shapes in pictures, e.g. bicycle wheels, houses, rooftops.

- Tell the story of *Mr Square*:

  - Mr Square lives in a square house. He has a square garden with a square tree and square flowers. He has a square dog called Boxy and he drives a square car.

  - You can, of course, make up other square things in Mr Square's life but beware of being too complicated. The children may have their own ideas.

- Ask the children to make a picture of Mr Square and some of the things mentioned in the story. If you have sets of different-sized stick-on shapes this would make this task easier and more accurate from a shape point of view.

- The same treatment can be given to Mrs Circle, Miss Triangle and Mr Star, remembering the gender can be anything.

- The children can choose which shape to use in their picture but encourage sticking to a single shape rather than making a picture containing random squares, circles, triangles and stars.

- Alternatively, the children could make a 'person-only' group, e.g. Mr Square, Mrs Star, Miss Circle and Little Baby Triangle.

Mystery Shape-in-a-Bag

EYFS Aspect	Resources	Group Size
Shape, Space & Measures	Large cloth bag Small and medium-sized familiar items of different shapes	1–4

- Secretly place several familiar objects in a large, cloth bag.

- Explain the rules of the game to the children:

  - Put a hand into the bag and take hold of an object.

  - Feel all round the object and try to guess what it is.

- Children take turns to make their guess. Encourage decision-making by asking what the edges are like, e.g. 'Does it have straight edges?/Are there any round/soft edges?'

- Once a guess is made, child removes the object to check if right or wrong.

- Place all the right guesses together and all the wrong guesses together. Discuss reasons for mistakes, if there were any.

- Count all the items at the end.

Safety Note

Beware small items and avoid really sharp edges.

Hello Mr Postman

EYFS Aspect	Resources	Group Size
Numbers as Labels and for Counting	Any dressing-up clothes for a postman Large envelopes, paper, colours Large numbers to identify 'houses'	1–4

- Mark envelopes 1–5 (or more if you like).

- Children write letters or draw pictures to go into envelopes.

- Children can choose which envelope to put their letter into and do so.

- Nominate a child as the postman, dressing him/her accordingly.

- Give large house numbers to the others in the group.

- The postman delivers the right envelope to the right house.

- The householder opens the envelope and reads the letter – this could be either talking about the picture or simply making up what the letter says and saying who it is from.

- To play again, the postman can be changed and the letters swapped around or new ones made.

Taking this further

If this is to be a regular game it can be more realistic with large doors made from giant cardboard boxes. Letterboxes can be cut into them and the numbers painted or fixed on. This could open the way to ringing or knocking to deliver an exciting parcel.

IDEA
94

Just a Minute – 1

EYFS Aspect	Resources	Group Size
Shape, Space & Measures	Tricycle or scooter Giant 1-minute sand timer	1–4

This is ideally an outside activity but it can be done in a large open hall.

- Show the children the 1-minute sand timer, explaining it always takes the same amount of time for the sand to go through. Let them concentrate for 1 minute as they watch it pour.

- Work out a reasonable 'lap' or safe course in the area available, allowing for no more than four or five laps to be coverable in the minute.

- Have the children take it in turns to complete as many laps as possible in the timed minute. Record the respective numbers plus landmarks reached when the time is up.

- Children can have more goes to try to beat their best.

Taking this further

Use any reasonable physical activity which can be counted easily.

Safety Note

Need to get the speed/safety balance right.

Just a Minute – 2

EYFS Aspect	Resources	Group Size
Calculating Shape, Space & Measures	Giant 1-minute timer	Any

The object of this activity is to enable the children to imagine and estimate 1 minute's duration . . . and it can be very quiet!

● The children should be sat well spread out in chairs, on cushions or on the floor.

● Show the timer and explain how it works. Let the children watch the sand go through a few times.

● Tell them the rules of the game:

– Everyone sits very still and quiet.

– When everyone is ready the timer will be turned to start the minute and the children cover their eyes.

– They have to imagine the minute passing and stand quietly when they think the time is up.

– The one who stands most recently before the time is up is the winner. (Unfortunately, you cannot have a winner just after the time is up because anyone left would naturally stand up as soon as 'time's up' is called.)

● When everyone is clear on the rules, begin the first minute.

● Play the game enough times to enable the children to improve on their timing.

Taking this further

• If you teach the children a rhyme which takes just a minute to say or can be recited two or three times in a minute, it will help them to judge the time more accurately; they can recite it in their heads.

• This game can also be played with walking over a given distance. The distance would be one which is easily walked in the minute at normal pace so the children would have to regulate the speed. It is very difficult to get young ones to maintain a steady pace, however, and they are likely to keep up with the fastest walkers.

IDEA 96

Take the Biscuit

EYFS Aspect	Resources	Group Size
Numbers as Labels and for Counting Calculating Shape, Space & Measures	Play dough (bought or home-made) Small, safe pastry cutters Rolling pin	1–4

- Provide enough play dough for each child to cut out up to ten biscuit shapes.

- Children roll out their play dough to a biscuit-thickness layer.

- Practise cutting biscuit shapes from the dough.

- When all the children are confident with the cutters, have them make their dough into a single lump again and roll it out once more.

- There are several number investigations you can bring out of this. Your choice will largely depend upon the ability and interest of the children. Here are some examples:

  – Ask the children to estimate how many biscuits of the same size can be cut from their dough. They then check their estimate. You will have to decide whether or not to include the in-between bits after the first cutting.

  – Use a range of different-sized cutters and talk about the relative numbers of biscuits you would get. Test out the estimates.

  – What difference does a thicker pastry make to the number of biscuits?

  – What's the thinnest pastry we can make?

  – With all the biscuits cut out, how many will each of us get if we shared them?

  – If you have four biscuits and you wanted to put two cherries on each (represented by red counters or large beads), how many cherries would you need?

– If we baked all these and we each ate one (take away one each), how many would be left (count remainder)?

 Taking this further

- Investigate differences in biscuit numbers between various fun-shaped pastry cutters, e.g. stars, gingerbread men, Santas.

- If you have facilities for real baking, you could try this with biscuit mix.

IDEA 97

Hide-and-Seek

EYFS Aspect	Resources	Group Size
Numbers as Labels and for Counting	Cuddly toy/s (for Option 2)	1–4

Option 1 – Play the traditional hide-and-seek game (if there is a suitable, safe environment, either indoors or out).

- Children take it in turns to be the seeker and hide their eyes while the others hide within the selected area.

- For the counting, there are a number of options all with which the adult may need to help all or some children:

  - Count to ten slowly

  - Count to ten slowly twice

  - Count to ten slowly and then from ten down to zero.

- Seeker says, 'Coming ready or not' and sets off in search of others.

- When all are found the game starts again with the next seeker.

Option 2 – 'Hiders' hide cuddly toys instead of themselves. Particularly useful if space or hiding places is restricted.

- Same rules and counting as Option 1.

Safety Note

The area chosen must be a safe one for children to be 'out of sight' if using Option 1.

IDEA 98

Where Am I?

EYFS Aspect	Resources	Group Size
Numbers as Labels and for Counting Calculating Shape, Space & Measures	Beanbag cushion seat or giant cuddly toy Blindfold	Any

- Begin with all the children in a large circle and, ideally, a beanbag cushion in the centre.

- Explain that the object of the game is to move, blindfolded, from the outside of the circle to the beanbag and sit on it. This will be done using instructions from the others in the circle.

- Choose a volunteer child and put on the blindfold.

- Make sure the child is happy and steady while temporarily unsighted. An adult should be alongside as a guide if necessary and to help with the directions and counting.

- Point the blindfolded child in whatever direction you like to start.

- Ask for directions from the group which will move the chosen one to the cushion in stages. NB The path does not have to be direct, it is more fun if it is not.

- When the child has successfully reached and sat on the beanbag, remove blindfold, clap and he or she returns to the circle.

- Choose another volunteer for the next go.

  A typical set of instructions could be:

  - [Child facing OUT from circle at start] *Turn round*

  - *Take three steps forward*

  - *Two steps sideways/left* (confident knowledge of left and right need not be a problem as next instruction can be *four steps the other way*).

- *Two tiny steps forward*

- *Small step backwards*

- *One step right*

- *Turn around*

- *Sit down!*

Taking this further

With a small group of children, set up a safe obstacle course. Children – sighted in this case – take it in turns to go through it on the instructions of the rest. This would involve a much wider vocabulary, e.g. *under, over, around, through, behind, between, inside.*

IDEA	
99	# Whatever Next?

EYFS Aspect	Resources	Group Size
Numbers as Labels and for Counting Shape, Space & Measures	Props for mimes (optional)	Any

The sequence of familiar activities and events can be shown by fun mime orchestration.

- Begin by talking about a typical day – the basic events from start to end – and then cover familiar morning activities in sequential order.

- Lots of personal hygiene and personal experience ideas will come from the children but quickly reduce it to five main activities in order:

  - Waking up
  - Washing
  - Dressing
  - Breakfast
  - Cleaning teeth.

- Invent mimes for each and rehearse with all the children in sequence.

- Introduce 'Mrs (or Mr) Funny' who does things in the wrong order, e.g. washes, wakes, cleans teeth, has breakfast, to show importance of sequence.

- Divide children into mime groups and allocate single mimes to each, using simple props if you wish.

- Direct the children through the mime sequence (not forgetting Mrs/Mr Funny).

  Alternative or additional sequences you can use are:

  - Taking out toys/playing with toys/tidying toys/wash hands/lunch

  - Going to the supermarket/shopping in trolley/shopping on the checkout/going home/shopping in larder.

 ## Taking this further

Make the mimes into a short play and add percussion or sound effects.

'Favouritest' Animals

EYFS Aspect	Resources	Group Size
Numbers as Labels and for Counting Calculating Shape, Space & Measures	Duplicate pictures of four different animals, e.g. stickers OR rubber stamps (You will need as many of each animal as there are children A2 size sheet of card or paper Four separate boxes to contain the stickers/stamps	10–12

The object of this activity is to construct a pictogram.

● Preparation:

– Decide which animals are going to be used for the children to select their favourite among them. This may be determined by the rubber stamps or stickers available; it could be farm animals if they have recently visited a farm or it could be domestic pets.

– Draw four columns or horizontal sections. NB Pictograms can be in vertical columns starting at the top or bottom or in horizontal lines starting from the left.

– Place the picture and name of each animal at the head/base of the columns.

– Give the chart a title, e.g. 'Our Favourite Animals'.

– Have the stickers or rubber stamps available.

● Discuss the animals chosen.

● Ask children to choose which one is their favourite and tell them everyone's choices can be shown in a picture.

● Call children one at a time to pick only one sticker (or rubber stamp) and place it appropriately in its column.

- The children will need help to start in the right place and keep the stickers fairly well and evenly spaced.

- When all children have placed a stamp or sticker help them interpret the data! Remind the children that each picture means a child's choice, e.g. 'Which column has the most stickers? Let's count and see. So our favourite pet is a [cat].'

- Any column without a choice is also important, e.g. 'Nobody has chosen mice as their favourite pet. Mice scores zero or none.'

Taking this further

- You can make a 3D pictogram for favourite colours by using interlocking or stacking bricks. The children simply add a brick of their favourite colour to the possible choices arranged in a row.

- Other themes can be used with a keyed shape element, e.g. 'Favourite Foods'. Label each column with a food picture (from magazine or supermarket advertisement). Allocate a different shaped sticker for each food. Child places the appropriate sticker in the correct column. 'Favourite Activities' is an interesting theme to try.